broth

broth

Nature's cure-all for health and nutrition,
with delicious recipes for broths, soups, stews and risottos

Vicki Edgson and Heather Thomas

Photography by Lisa Linder

jacqui
small

First published in 2016 by
Jacqui Small LLP
74–77 White Lion Street
London N1 9PF

Publisher: Jacqui Small
Managing Editor: Emma Heyworth-Dunn
Designer: Maggie Town
Editor: Daniel Hurst
Food Stylist: Jennifer Joyce
Assistant Food Stylist: Emma Godwin
Production: Maeve Healy

ISBN: 978 1 910254 48 6

A catalogue record for this book is
available from the British Library.

2018 2017 2016

10 9 8 7 6 5 4 3 2 1

Printed in China

Contents

INTRODUCTION

FROM BROTH TO BRODO

Broths, stocks and brodos – as the Italians lovingly call them – have been used as the cornerstones of some of the world's best-loved dishes for hundreds of years, but recently there has been a growing realization that these simple-seeming mainstays of every chef's kitchen are, in fact, nutritional powerhouses that contain the building blocks of good health.

Now, more than ever, we are placing increased value on foods that are cooked from scratch at home and we're turning back to the basics from which our food traditions originate. The last 20 years have been dominated by a food culture centred around speed and convenience, but this legacy has left us with rising rates of diabetes and obesity, which we are only just starting to address. This newfound awareness of the importance of good nutrition and the impact on our health of what we put into our bodies is leading more of us back into the kitchen, happy to invest our time and effort to ensure that what we're feeding ourselves and our families is not only delicious but also nutritionally sound; the rising popularity of bone broth is clear evidence of this trend.

In the following pages, we show you how making your own broths from scratch can transform your entire culinary repertoire, and, with very little effort on your part, you can be confident that the dishes you cook are packed with healthy, life-enhancing nutrients. And for those of you with a busy work schedule and lifestyle, broths can be made in large batches, frozen and defrosted as needed, so you never again have to reach for a stock (bouillon) cube. The sheer scale and variety of dishes that you can make from them is truly astounding and the flavour is so superior to the commercial alternatives.

From fresh-tasting soups and warming stews to creamy-textured, unctuous risottos and fragrant curries, the easy-to-follow recipes in this book are full of flavour, look great and will make you feel good. You don't require any specialist skills and it's especially reassuring to know that you are creating something as nourishing to your body as it is to your soul.

Make broth your herbal medicine

Whether consumed on their own or used within the recipes featured later in this book, broths are among the most nutritious foods you can eat, full of amino acids and minerals. Listed below are some of the key ways you can utilize broth to improve your overall health as well as information on how it can augment your existing diet.

GUT HEALTH

A weak intestinal lining, or 'leaky gut', can lead to food particles being absorbed directly into the blood stream, resulting in immune or intolerant reactions as well as being an access point for viruses and bacteria. The collagen released when making bone broth has an amazing ability to repair the endothelial tissue (the lining of the small and large intestine), but vitamin C has to be present for maximum absorption into the skin tissue. Because of this, if you are using bone broth to improve the health of your gut, it's best to combine it with potatoes, bell peppers and beetroot (beets), along with garlic or onions, which are rich in methionine, an amino acid that helps to rebuild skin tissue of all kinds; dishes such as Thai red beef curry soup (see page 62) or Gulyas (see page 92) would be ideal for this.

BONE HEALTH

Bone broths are packed with calcium and magnesium, both of which are essential for bone repair. Calcium is the most abundant mineral in the human body, but if you don't get enough of it from the food you eat your body will use the reserves stored in your bones to maintain normal cell function, leading eventually to weakened bones and possible osteoporosis. Magnesium works hand-in-hand with calcium, as it allows your body to uptake and absorb it into the bones. Without magnesium, excess calcium deposits will not be assimilated in the correct way and they can end up in the lining of delicate arteries, contributing to atherosclerosis and subsequently heart disease.

ANTI-INFLAMMATORY EFFECTS

Many of the minerals and amino acids found in bone broth possess anti-inflammatory properties and, as such, can help with the prevention and treatment of many illnesses. In particular, chondroitin sulphates (a structural component of cartilage), glucosamine, zinc, calcium and magnesium are vital for reducing inflammatory effects within your body, which are now recognized as one of the main causes of illnesses such as irritable bowel syndrome (IBS), asthma and psoriasis.

HAIR, SKIN AND NAILS

The human body is very clever at finding the resources it needs to stay healthy. Because of this, essential nutrients and minerals are often 'borrowed' from our less vital organs, such as nails, skin and hair, when the body is going through times of healing or repair. Collagen, fibrinogen and elastin are found mainly in bone broths, rather than vegetable ones, and can help to top up any deficiencies and repair the damage that has been done.

BROTH TO SUPPLEMENT DIET

Owing to their rich nutrient content, broths can work in a number of ways to enhance your diet. The bone broths can be used within a healthy weight-loss plan to ensure you are getting the most complex source of amino acids to promote your general wellbeing. They are also a superb way to manage fasting-style diets as they are relatively low in calories while providing a plethora of vital nutrients. In addition, they are perfect on any low-GI plan, being rich in protein, which helps to balance blood sugar levels – this also makes them especially useful if you're following the 5:2 diet. And because they are so nutrient-dense and make use of the bones and carcasses of animals that most people throw away, they make good sense for people on the Paleo diet, too. The essential nine amino acids are all required for the production of energy at a cellular level, making bone broth a good way to enhance athletic performance, stamina and endurance-based diets.

The health benefits of broth

As I've already stated, broth has remarkable health-giving properties and it's packed with vital nutrients that our bodies need to repair themselves and to stay healthy at a cellular level. At specific times of their life cycle, our systems crave different nutrients to fulfil a wide range of functions. Outlined below are the ways in which drinking and cooking with broth can help support and promote your health, as well as your family's, at every stage of life.

BABIES

Broth of any kind is never a replacement for a mother's breast milk or for formula. However, as babies grow older and start being weaned onto solids, it's worth considering adding some freshly-made chicken broth, or other bone broth, to their diet. It's packed with vital amino acids, which are the building blocks of protein, and when these are combined with calcium, magnesium, boron and manganese, they help in the formation of strong bones. As well as being rich in all these minerals, broth contains high levels of zinc, which is needed for building a healthy immune system, especially at this early stage in a baby's life.

As you start to wean your baby onto his first solids, adding a little of any of the animal broths will provide excellent nutrients for promoting growth, immunity and healthy gut development. It's a good idea to purée the broth with root vegetables, such as carrots, sweet potato, swede (rutabaga) and parsnip. They are a good source of antioxidants and have a natural sweetness that is appealing to a baby trying out new flavours. In addition to the bone broths, you may also use the Vegetable top and tail broth (see page 51), but the Allium broth (see page 55) has too strong a taste for a young palate and can cause wind or even colic in some babies with under-developed digestive systems.

Once he is fully weaned, there is no reason why your baby can't enjoy a cup of bone broth several times a day – be led by him and you can't go wrong.

CHILDREN

The changes that take place in a child's brain development during the first 10 years of life are the most rapid and complex in their life cycle. During this time it's essential that their diet is high in both omega-3 and -6 essential fatty acids, as these are the vital carriers that encourage the connectivity of messaging between one nerve cell and another; this is very important for the healthy development of learning, memory and concentration. These fatty acids are found most abundantly in fish (especially oily fish, such as sardines and mackerel) and shellfish, so try introducing these into your child's diet to ensure he is getting everything he needs for his mental development. Both the White fish bone broth (see page 43) and Shellfish broth (see page 47), and their related dishes in this book, are a great way of obtaining omega-3 and especially its bio-active components EPA and DHA (eicosapentaenoic and doxosahexaenoic acids), which are the richest and most important sources of all.

If your child dislikes or cannot tolerate seafood, don't worry – omega-nutrition is present in all meat, poultry and game bone broth, although to a lesser degree.

ADOLESCENTS

In addition to brain food, all children and adolescents require ample protein for skeletal development as their bodies are continuously growing and developing throughout childhood and puberty – all the animal broths are ideal for this. Teenage girls also require abundant sources of magnesium to support their hormonal development as it starts to evolve and menstruation begins. The Vegetable top and tail broth (see page 51) is a rich source of magnesium-laden vegetables and can be used in a variety of soups, stews, casseroles, rice and grain dishes. And, as boys' hormones change, their testes drop and their sex drive amplifies, their need for zinc increases – it is an essential requirement for sperm production. Fish, shellfish, beef and chicken bone broths all supply plenty of zinc.

PREGNANCY

At no point during a woman's life is the nutritional content of her food more important than when she is pregnant. During this time your body focuses on providing your unborn child with all the nutrients that are essential for his development, even at the expense of your own health – for example, if you're not getting sufficient calcium, your body will take it from your bones to give your growing child what he needs, thereby making your bones more unhealthy and brittle.

As protein provides the essential amino acids for development and growth, it's important that you have some at every meal. Drinking a supplementary cup of bone broth (chicken, beef, ham hock or fish) will supply a rich source of protein without having to consume large amounts of meat. This is especially useful if you are feeling nauseous or unwell.

During pregnancy, it's vital that you balance your blood sugar levels throughout the day. Doing this helps to maintain lasting energy during what can be a very exhausting time, especially if this is not your first baby and other children are making demands on your time. Eating family-friendly meals with protein-rich bone broths as their base is a great way of satisfying hunger, not only for you and your children but also your unborn child, whilst helping to prevent morning sickness. Good meals from this book to try would be Chilean pork cazuela (see page 103), Chicken cacciatore with white bean smash (see page 108) and Griddled chicken with scented lemon couscous (see page 141). If you're vegetarian, you can add some nori seaweed, beans and pulses, nuts and seeds to your broth, soup or risotto to boost the protein content.

You can substitute your usual late-night drink with a cup of bone broth, either on its own or with some added flavourings. This helps to ensure that your unborn child is getting the calcium needed for healthy ligament, cartilage and teeth development while not sacrificing your own supply.

And it's good to continue drinking broth during the postnatal period, too, when you're recovering from the birth, looking after your new baby and you need to drink a lot of liquid throughout the day to stimulate your breast milk. It's also convenient and highly nutritious when you're feeling tired or don't have much time to cook.

MENOPAUSE

Many women don't even realize that they are experiencing the onset of menopause, as they may associate some of the symptoms with those of aging: temperature fluctuations (hot flushes), loss of sex drive, and skin texture and hair changes are all easy to miss or ignore when you're dealing with the pressures of everyday life. For some unfortunate women, the symptoms are more serious and pronounced, including forgetfulness, lack of focus and concentration, and even low-grade depression and loss of identity. However, there's no need to despair: all of these symptoms are related to hormonal fluctuations and can be ameliorated by consuming the essential fatty acids found in meat, poultry, fish and shellfish broths. The realization that a cup of simple bone broth can help regulate our hormones as well as providing us with a hot, nutritious drink is one of the key reasons, we believe, for its recent surge in popularity.

As well as helping to manage our hormones (or, certainly, reducing sudden fluctuations in their levels), the essential fatty acids found in animal bone broth also play a role in regulating nerve function and neuronal connectivity in the brain, aiding the maintenance of a good memory and lessening the likelihood of anxiety and depression in later years. And another benefit is that these fatty acids help to maintain skin integrity and elasticity, so we look younger for longer.

LATER LIFE

During later life, especially beyond the age of 70, our body presents us with a whole new set of problems, especially digestive ones. These often appear when the delicate lining of the intestine starts to thin, which can lead to 'leaky gut'. If you have this condition, your body's intolerant reactions to what were previously acceptable foods can increase because they are released more readily into the blood stream. Drinking and cooking with bone broth can be very therapeutic – the collagen it contains is vital for helping strengthen the lining of the digestive tract. The flipside of this thinning of the lining of the gut is that it's easier for the body to digest and assimilate amino acids, which, in turn, help to balance blood sugar levels and provide you with more energy throughout the day. At this time in life, look for simple foods that taste delicious and provide an abundance of antioxidants together with protein for maximum potency: Aegean fish soup (see page 75) and Tuscan bean and vegetable soup with Parmesan crisps (see page 80) are both good options, as are Spelt with wild mushrooms (see page 142) and all the risottos. On a practical note, if you are preparing food for an elderly relative, focus on dishes that can be prepared in bulk and frozen in individual portions. These help to promote independence while guaranteeing good nutrition.

Make it a rule to eat 'light at night': by keeping your evening meal light and not eating too late, you are less likely to experience heartburn, indigestion and disturbed sleep, and your blood sugar levels will stay constant. The old maxim of breakfast like a king, lunch like a prince and dine like a pauper still holds true. Always eat a good breakfast and lunch as you need these sources of energy for boosting movement and thought throughout the day, but just a cup of broth or light soup in the evening is sufficient.

Bones, ligaments and cartilage are more brittle at this stage of life, so bone broth provides bone-supporting nutrients (see the chart opposite) to help prevent tears, fractures and osteoarthritis. Eat at least three dishes containing bone broth per week – this goes a long way towards protecting these increasingly delicate tissues.

NUTRIENT	REQUIRED FOR	FOUND IN
PROTEIN	All healing, rebuilding and repair, regeneration of all tissues in the body, blood sugar regulation.	● ● ● ● ● ● ● ●
COLLAGEN	All skin, internal and external; all ligaments, cartilage and bone matrix; integrity of the endothelial lining of the colon for proper absorption.	● ● ● ● ● ● ● ●
CALCIUM	Formation of all bone, ligaments and cartilage, nails, hair and teeth; cardiovascular health (contraction of heart muscle), peristalsis of the colon, nerve connectivity from and to the brain, metabolism.	● ● ● ● ● ● ● ●
MAGNESIUM	Absorption of calcium into bone, relaxation of muscle (e.g. heart muscle, arteries and colon/bowel); nerve transmission and communication, eyesight, metabolism, thyroid function; management of stress, mood, anxiety and depression; energy production; relief from fatigue; relief from headaches and migraines, reduction of postmenstrual syndrome.	● ● ● ● ● ● ● ● ● ●
ZINC	Protein breakdown into the amino acid building blocks, which occurs in the stomach through the production of gastric intrinsic factor; metabolic function through the thyroid; energy production; immunity; sexual hormone health, mood, reduction of anxiety and depression and increase of motivation; resistance to infections and viruses; natural growth, healing and repair	● ● ● ● ● ● ● ●
OMEGA-3	Cell integrity, anti inflammatory (all types – skin, heart, lungs), brain and cognitive function, memory and concentration; balancing blood sugar levels, energy production, production of hormones; regulation of metabolism; weight management.	● ● ●
POTASSIUM	Regulation of heartbeat, nerve transmission, kidney function, acuity of all the senses (sight, taste, touch, sound and smell), intra-cellular sodium regulation (sweat, oedema, cellulite and other puffiness or pooling of skin such as swollen ankles, fingers and wrists), food intolerances, skin reactions.	● ● ● ● ●

KEY TO SYMBOLS: 1 Classic beef bone broth **2** Rich marrow bone broth
3 Light chicken broth **4** Dark rich chicken broth **5** Ham hock broth **6** Game broth
7 White fish bone broth **8** Shellfish broth **9** Vegetable top and tail broth **10** Allium broth

① ② ③ ④ ⑤ ⑥ ⑦ ⑧ ⑨ ⑩

THE ESSENTIAL BROTHS

In an age when many are eschewing animal protein in favour of its vegetarian alternatives, there are some sources of protein that simply can't be ignored, providing they are sourced from grass-fed animals that are reared and treated humanely. Whilst vegetarian proteins are superb in themselves, they rarely supply the abundance of amino acids required for rebuilding and repair. Broth made from beef bones is mineral-rich and contains complete re-building nutrients vital to those who wish to pursue a natural anti-ageing approach to their health, without resorting to facial fillers and other synthetic methods to creating a youthful look. The collagen found in the marrow of bone broth is far more bio-available to the body than any supplement alternative or cosmetic injectable facial treatment, and works with the body's natural repairing systems over a longer period of time.

Classic beef bone broth

MAKES APPROX. 1.2 LITRES/2 PINTS

1.5 kg/3 lb 3 oz beef bones (T-bone and knuckle work well) cut into 5 cm/2 in pieces

2 sticks celery, roughly chopped

2 medium carrots (parsnips or swede (rutabaga) would also work well), roughly chopped

2 medium onions, roughly chopped

1 mixed bunch thyme, sage and marjoram, tied together with string

2.25 litres/4 pints water

4 tbsp apple cider or red wine vinegar

ground black pepper

1 Preheat the oven to 190°C/375°F/gas mark 5. Spread the chopped bones over a large roasting sheet and transfer to the oven to cook for 45–50 minutes until well browned and sticking to the tray. Add a splash of water to the pan and stir to loosen the bones and remove any congealed juices. Transfer the bones to a large pan.

2 Place all the vegetables and herbs in the pan and pour over enough of the water to cover. Add the vinegar and a generous grinding of black pepper, then cover the pan and bring to the boil. Reduce to a gentle simmer and leave to cook, covered, for 12–24 hours, regularly topping up the water to ensure it is always covering the bones. The longer the broth cooks, the richer it will be.

3 Cool the broth to room temperature, then strain through a piece of muslin (cheesecloth) into a large bowl. Use the broth immediately or portion it into freezer-proof containers and store in the fridge for 5 days or the freezer for up to 5 months.

A classic beef bone broth is the essential ingredient in Pho, a Vietnamese clear soup of beef broth flavoured with fresh root ginger, coconut, sugar, fish sauce, sliced spring onions (scallions), chillies and spices (a cinnamon stick, coriander and fennel seeds, whole cloves and star anise). Add thinly sliced grilled steak, some cooked rice noodles, lime juice and chopped herbs – coriander (cilantro), mint and basil – just before serving. Delicious! You can make this with rich marrow bone broth, too.

Now try this...

- This broth can be reheated to make a wonderful fortifying drink – at any time of the day it's a great pick-me-up.

- For a dish that's a little closer to home, richly flavoured beef broth is clarified with egg whites and then strained to make a clear consommé.

This is a far richer and yet lighter-coloured stock than the Classic beef bone broth (page 18), and requires that you drain the fat from the bones after roasting them and prior to simmering for the broth. However, it is a far richer source of two amino acids associated with growth, healing and repair – proline and glycine – , as well as a rich source of minerals and collagen to encourage bone resorption, the process where minerals are released from the bone, and skin renewal. Glycine further supports the body's natural detoxification and wound healing abilities. Proline is known for strengthening cell structures throughout the body, in particular the lining of the gut, to improve overall gut health.

Rich marrow bone broth

MAKES APPROX. 1.2 LITRES/2 PINTS

3 kg/6 lb 8 oz beef marrow bones (ask your butcher for bones chopped into 5 cm/2 in rounds for easier cooking)

2.25 litres/4 pints water

125 ml/4 fl oz/generous 1 cup apple cider vinegar

2 medium red onions, chopped

4 large carrots, roughly chopped

5 sticks celery, roughly chopped

2 leeks, trimmed and chopped

3 bay leaves

1 bouquet garni

a pinch of paprika/cayenne pepper

1

2

1 Preheat the oven to 190°C/375°F/gas mark 5. Spread the chopped marrow bones in a large roasting pan and transfer to the oven to cook for 45 minutes, allowing the fat to drain out of the bones and into the pan. Drain off the fat into a jug and set aside.

2 Place the bones in a large saucepan, together with the water, vinegar, vegetables, herbs and spices. Bring to a rolling boil, before reducing the heat to a gentle simmer.

3 Simmer for between 24–36 hours, turning off overnight for safety. Skim the residual fat and other debris that rise to the surface, then simmer for a further 20 minutes to richen and darken the broth.

4 Allow to cool completely. Strain through a fine sieve lined with a muslin (cheesecloth) to clarify. Store in the fridge for 5–6 days, or freeze immediately for future use.

You can drink this broth **on its own** but a **simple,** delicious and **highly nutritious** alternative would be to **poach an egg** in boiling water and lower it into a serving of the **broth,** in which you can **wilt** some **baby spinach** or **watercress.**

Now try this...

■ Alternatively, you can heat some of the broth in a small pan and break an egg into it. Cook at a gentle simmer until the white of the egg is firm, but the yolk is still soft. This delicious dish makes a perfect breakfast or light meal.

■ This broth is so useful in healthy cooking, so keep some handy in a container in the refrigerator or freezer and use for cooking quinoa or nutty brown rice, or even steaming and braising vegetables. It can also be used for making brown sauces or gravy to go with roast beef or lamb, plus is great in oxtail stews and hearty beef soups.

! Beef bones packed with marrow can yield quite an intense (and often lingering) odour when being cooked for hours on top of the hob (stovetop). You may wish to cook this in a heavy casserole inside the oven, as it is far less pungent and doesn't need to interfere with any other cooking that you may wish to do at the same time. Alternatively, you could cook this in a pressure cooker to save time.

Not many would consider making a broth from a ham hock, and yet it is both delicious and an abundant source of marrow. You can buy ham hock bones from your butcher who has cut away virtually all the ham-on-the-bone, and who will usually discard the bone altogether. Most butchers will just give you these. If you have ever cooked Osso Buco (page 96), with veal bones, you know how tasty the marrow is from these bones, and the ham hock broth is similar. I have been known to smear the marrow straight onto the best spelt or rye toast and eat it with simply a splash of lemon juice – delicious brain food, which you won't be able to buy in the store!

Ham hock broth

MAKES APPROX. 1.2 LITRES/2 PINTS

1 kg/2 lb 4 oz or 2 medium ham hock bones with meat removed or a little meat left on them

2.25 litres/4 pints water

2 large red onions, roughly chopped

4 sticks celery, roughly chopped

3 medium carrots, chopped

2 bay leaves

1 bunch thyme or parsley (or both)

1 tsp coriander or cumin seeds

10 black peppercorns

2 portobello mushrooms, sliced

1 Preheat the oven to 190°C/375°F/gas mark 5. Spread the ham hock bones in a large roasting pan and transfer to the oven to cook for 45 minutes, allowing the fat to drain out of the bones and into the pan. Lower the oven temperature to 180°C/350°F/gas mark 4.

2 Transfer the bones to a heavy ovenproof casserole dish (Dutch oven), and pour over the water. Add the remaining ingredients, cover, and bring to the boil over a high heat. Once boiling, transfer to the oven and leave to cook, covered, for 4–5 hours.

3 Remove from the oven, allow to cool, then strain the stock through a double sieve (strainer) into a container. Store in the fridge overnight, then remove any fat from the top of stock before using. This can be kept in the fridge for up to 6 days, or frozen for up to 3 months.

You can make a great Chinese clear soup by adding shredded leftover roast pork, chilli, soy sauce, spring onions (scallions) and pak choi (bok choy) to some simmering ham hock broth.

Now try this...

■ The most common way of using ham broth is in a split pea and ham soup, but it's great in soups made with spring greens, fresh or frozen peas and mint, or even lentils.

■ You can substitute ham hock broth for chicken broth in a variety of soups, stews and casseroles that use pork or sausages. It is also delicious when added to many Chinese pork dishes and clear soups.

Think of every culinary remedy known to your grandmother (and she didn't need to be Jewish to know the healing properties of chicken) and, without a doubt, your list will have started with chicken soup. The mineral content of chicken bones, especially zinc, is superb for supporting the immune system in helping to combat simple fatigue-related illnesses right through to major illness. Chicken broth is the panacea we have all sought, and always had at our side. My own mother never disposed of a chicken carcass without having made a broth first, and I have followed suit. I believe that it is the regular consumption of chicken broth in my soups and stews that has allowed me to age gracefully without the use of facial fillers and plumpers, as the abundant collagen released in broth-making has served me so well. Try it and see for yourself.

Light chicken broth

1

MAKES APPROX. 1.2 LITRES/2 PINTS

2 chicken carcasses weighing at least 500 g/
1 lb 2 oz each

2 leeks, trimmed and chopped

3 medium spring onions (scallions)

2 cloves garlic

1 thumb-sized piece root ginger, peeled and grated

1 thumb-sized piece root turmeric, peeled and sliced

1 tsp red or black peppercorns.

1 sprig thyme, oregano or bay leaf,
according to taste

1 bunch parsley

2.25 litres/4 pints water

1 Put the chicken carcasses in a large heavy-based pan with the remaining ingredients and bring to the boil.

2 Cover the pan and reduce the heat to a simmer for 40–50 minutes. Turn off the heat and allow to cool slightly.

3 Skim off any froth or fat that has risen to the surface.

4 Strain through a fine sieve, pressing all the juice out of the bones and vegetables. Discard the vegetables and herbs.

5 Allow the broth to cool before transferring to the fridge and leaving overnight. Skim any congealed fat off the top of the broth in the morning and the broth is ready to use. It will keep in the fridge for 5–6 days or can be frozen in batches for future use.

4

Make a **quick gazpacho** on a hot day by blitzing some ripe **tomatoes, red (bell) peppers, garlic, cucumber,** a few glugs of **fruity olive oil** and a spoonful or two of **sherry vinegar** with some cold **chicken broth** plus some white **bread** that's been soaked in cold water for 20 minutes. **Blend** until **smooth** and you have the desired consistency, then pass through a **sieve** and refrigerate until **chilled.** Serve topped with **diced tomato, peppers, cucumber** and **parsley.**

Now try this...

- This is probably the most versatile broth you can make – it has so many uses. Perhaps it is best known as the base for chicken noodle soup (or 'Jewish penicillin', as it is affectionately known, owing to its high zinc content, which supports the immune system), nutritious and restorative when you're feeling ill and have lost your appetite. Cook some chopped onion, leek, carrot and celery until tender in the simmering broth. Stir in some shredded cooked chicken and add at least a handful of vermicelli pasta. Simmer gently until the pasta is cooked and tender, then season with salt and pepper and add plenty of chopped curly parsley.

- Many Asian hot and sour soups are made with chicken broth as are vegetable and bean soups, or you could simply stir a couple of spoonfuls of miso paste into simmering broth for a comforting Japanese soup. An iced summer gazpacho is transformed by substituting chicken broth for water.

- The Italians have a mean way with chicken broth, which is deceptively simple: to make Stracciatella, they whisk some eggs with finely grated Parmesan and drizzle it into a pan of simmering chicken broth while stirring gently with a fork to separate the egg mixture into long thin strands – this takes about 2 minutes. Chopped parsley and some shredded spinach are added, plus a dash of lemon juice just before serving.

- A good way to use up the leftover chicken and vegetables from the Sunday roast is to add them to some hot chicken broth and when everything is heated through, blitz it in batches in a blender. Check the seasoning and serve as a soup.

- You can cook rice, grain or even polenta in chicken broth or use it for braising vegetables. Add simmering broth to risotto a ladleful at a time, or boiling broth to couscous, then cover and leave to soak.

This is a far richer and darker stock for those dishes that require a fuller taste, as the bones are roasted prior to simmering, which changes the colour and enriches the flavour of the stock. In Italy, where they still cook capons (male birds), they tend to use their bones for their broth as this creates an earthier, richer stock. If you know a local chicken farmer who is willing to sell you his capons, try this recipe with one – it pays to source them!

Dark rich chicken broth

MAKES APPROX. 1.2 LITRES/2 PINTS

10–12 chicken leg and wing bones (or leg bones only)

2.25 litres/4 pints water

2 red onions, unpeeled and quartered

2 garlic cloves, crushed

1 stick celery, chopped

1 carrot, unpeeled and chopped

2 bay leaves

5 sprigs thyme or marjoram

1 tsp coriander seeds

½ tsp fennel seeds

10 red or black peppercorns

sea salt, to taste

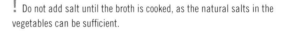

! Do not add salt until the broth is cooked, as the natural salts in the vegetables can be sufficient.

1 Preheat the oven to 180°C/350°F/gas mark 4. Spread the chicken bones over a large baking sheet and transfer to the oven to cook for 25–30 minutes until golden and crispy.

2 Place the bones in a large saucepan, together with remaining ingredients. Bring to a rolling boil, before reducing the heat to a gentle simmer and leaving to cook, covered, for 3–4 hours until the bones are soft and leaching their marrow into the broth. Skim the surface to remove any fatty chunks and set the broth aside to cool.

3 Strain the broth through a fine colander and discard the vegetables. Transfer the broth to the fridge for at least 2 hours until the broth has set to a jelly-like consistency.

4 Turn the jellied broth out into a bowl and remove any sediment that has gathered at its base. The broth is now ready to use and will keep in the fridge for 5–6 days or in the freezer for up to 3 months. To use the broth, transfer to a pan and heat to return it to a liquid consistency.

For a **refreshing detox** drink, heat some chicken broth in a pan and add a selection of **flavourings,** such as grated or shredded fresh **root ginger,** a lemongrass stalk, some chopped coriander (cilantro), turmeric root and Thai **mint,** together with a good squeeze of **lime juice.** For more heat, you can add some diced **chilli.**

Now try this...

- This richer version of a chicken bone broth is perfect for using in robust stews and casseroles or for making lighter versions of brown sauces that were traditionally made with beef bone broth, especially Espagnole and Bordelaise.

- Dark chicken broth is great for making gravy, giving it a much more intense flavour than the lighter broth. Stir it with some white wine or Marsala into the residues left in the pan after roasting the chicken, scraping up all the tasty bits sticking to the bottom of the pan, and then boil until reduced. You can add some redcurrant, quince or apple jelly, if you like, for a hint of sweetness.

If you were brought up with the spoils of the land when the hunting season is at its height, you will know that freezers inevitably end up with a stock of birds that are never eaten and which don't tend to last from one year to the next. The best use for these birds is to make delicious broths that can be used to enrich other dishes, making them more succulent and moist than they would be if cooked on their own. Being wild, these birds don't tend to have much fat on them, but they do have plenty of collagen in the marrow of their bones, which makes them all the more worthwhile from a nutritional point of view.

Game broth

MAKES APPROX. 1.2 LITRES/2 PINTS

1.5–2 kg/3 lb 5 oz–4 lb 8 oz oven-ready game birds, such as pheasant, partridge, quail or grouse (any combination will work, as long as the birds weren't too 'high' when they were frozen)

2 tbsp sunflower oil

2 medium onions, roughly chopped

4 shallots, trimmed and quartered

3 smoked garlic cloves, unpeeled

2.25 litres/4 pints water

2 large carrots, roughly sliced

2 sticks celery, roughly sliced

4 cloves

3 bay leaves

1 tsp black peppercorns

1 Preheat the oven to 190°C/375°F/gas mark 5. If the birds were previously frozen, ensure they are thoroughly defrosted. Use a sharp knife or cleaver to divide the birds into halves or quarters to ensure that they are all roughly the same size.

2 Place the birds in a large roasting pan and drizzle over the sunflower oil, using your hands to ensure they are well coated. Add the onions, shallots and garlic to the pan and transfer to the oven for 30 minutes until the birds are cooked. Strip the flesh from the bones, retaining the bones and setting the flesh aside for use in another dish.

3 Place the bones, together with the cooked onions, shallots and garlic, into a large heavy-based pan and add enough water to cover. Add the remaining ingredients and bring to the boil over a high heat. Once boiling, reduce the heat to a gentle simmer and leave to cook, covered, for 3–4 hours, until rich and dark, checking occasionally and topping up the water if necessary.

4 Once cooked, strain the broth and discard the bones and vegetables. Leave the broth to cool, then transfer to the fridge until ready to use. This will keep in the fridge for 5–6 days or in the freezer for up to 3 months.

Add **diced root vegetables** and **onions** plus **lentils, pearl barley** or **spelt** and some **shredded greens** to make a really **earthy, rustic** broth.

Now try this...

■ Game broth tastes fabulous reheated as a hot drink – in fact, it's so good that it's my favourite of all the broths.

■ Of course, it's perfect in game stews and casseroles or for making gravy to serve with roast pheasant or venison, or even venison sausages or a game toad in the hole. It can also be used in a Bolognese sauce with minced pork or wild boar and tossed with cooked pasta.

In many restaurants, the white sauces found in fish dishes are made from fish heads and bones. In some countries, especially throughout the Caribbean and Asia, fish heads, spines and tails are largely considered to be the most nutritious parts of the fish and are often eaten as dishes in their own right. In Greece, the cooked fish head is often served standing in the centre of a plate or bowl to be fought over for its nutritionally rich flesh. Pescetarians, who eat fish but not meat or poultry, can derive as much nutritional benefit from fish broths as those made from meat or poultry, with fish broths being especially high in nutrients that are essential for eye, skin, heart and brain health. This broth can be made in bulk as it freezes well and will transform even the simplest of dishes into something absolutely delicious.

White fish bone broth

MAKES APPROX. 1.2 LITRES/2 PINTS

1 kg/2 lb 4 oz heads, spines and tails of any white fish (sea bass, bream, haddock, cod, hake or haddock would all work well)

6 shallots, halved

6 sticks celery, finely sliced

3 star anise

1 large bunch parsley

1 large bulb fennel, including leaves and stalks, chopped lengthways

2 large carrots, sliced into rounds

2 onions, chopped

2 garlic cloves, unpeeled and sliced

250 ml/9 fl oz/generous 1 cup dry white wine (optional)

2.25 litres/4 pints water

salt and freshly ground black pepper, to taste

! Do NOT include smoked fish bones, as the resulting broth will be far too salty. Remember to wash all fish thoroughly and cut out all fish gills from the heads, as they are filled with blood.

1 Put the fish heads, spines (broken in half if too long) and tails into a large heavy-based saucepan, pile in all the other ingredients, then cover with the water.

2 Bring to the boil, turn down the heat, and simmer gently for 2–3 hours.

3 Leave to cool, if you wish, for a stronger flavour before straining out all the bones, vegetables and herbs, through a muslin (cheesecloth) lined sieve (strainer) for a crystal clear broth.

4 Store in the fridge for 3–4 days or freeze in batches for up to 3 months.

You can make a great miso broth by adding miso paste, chopped spring onions (scallions), chopped thin asparagus stems, wakame seaweed and chunks of tofu to some simmering fish broth.

Now try this...

■ For a really quick and easy fish soup, flavour the simmering broth with soy sauce or nam pla (Thai fish sauce) and lime juice and poach some white fish fillets in it. Stir in some chopped coriander (cilantro) or basil plus cooked egg or rice noodles for a more filling meal.

■ Using fish broth intensifies the flavour of a seafood risotto or paella. To make paella, you will need a really wide, shallow pan. Start off by frying chopped onions, garlic, peppers and some smoked paprika, then add some short-grain rice (Spanish Bomba or Calasparra) and cook for a couple of minutes before pouring in the fish broth and some saffron strands. Bring to the boil, then reduce the heat and simmer for at least 10 minutes before adding a selection of fish and/or seafood (mussels, prawns, squid, etc.) and cooking for a further 10 minutes or so until the fish is cooked and the rice is tender. For extra flavour, you can add wine, peas, green beans, fresh white lima beans, broad beans and parsley. In Spain, chorizo and chicken thighs are sometimes added, too.

■ Freeze the fish broth in labelled containers and use for making bouillabaisse or zuppa di pesce, its Italian equivalent. Recipes vary according to the region and fish available, so you don't have to follow them slavishly. Use whatever fish or shellfish you have to hand and simmer in the broth with tomatoes, onions, garlic, olive oil, herbs and red or white wine. Mop up the juices with some crusty bread or, if serving as a main course, add some potatoes.

In order to ensure that there is no risk associated with food allergies and intolerances, we recommend that you do not include prawn (shrimp) shells, as these tend to provoke allergic reactions more than most. The same can be said for mussels, as it is difficult to know which are safe until you have cooked them, but you can include these if you have had some yourself, and have saved only those that didn't 'rise to the surface' or remained unopen in the original cooking. Using lobster, crab and crayfish shells is ideal, and if your fishmonger prepares shellfish salads for his other clients, ask him to harvest and save these shells for you. This is a rich broth, but does make the relevant dish they are used in very tasty, as well as supplying an excellent source of calcium, which is especially beneficial for those people who tend to struggle to keep their levels up (see The health benefits of broth, pages 12–15).

Shellfish broth

MAKES APPROX. 1.2 LITRES/2 PINTS

4 tbsp light olive oil (or 2 tbsp coconut oil)

1 large red onion, finely diced

1 large garlic clove, peeled and finely diced

1 stick celery

1 thumbnail-sized piece root ginger, peeled and finely sliced

1 stick lemongrass (optional), smashed at the bulb end to release oils

1 kg/2 lb 4 oz mixed crustacean shells (crab, lobster, crayfish)

2.25 litres/4 pints water

1 small chilli, deseeded and finely chopped/or tiny pinch of saffron strands (both of these options add a hint of pink to the broth, as well as adding spice)

6–8 red peppercorns

1 small bunch thyme

1 Heat the oil in a large casserole dish (Dutch oven), then add the onion, garlic, celery, ginger and lemongrass (if using) and sweat for 3-4 minutes before adding the rest of the ingredients.

2 Add enough water to cover the shells, cover with a lid and turn the heat up to high. Bring to the boil.

3 Turn the heat down to a gentle simmer. Cook for 35-60 minutes until the aroma is seeping through the lid of the pan.

4 Turn off the heat, remove the lid, and allow to cool before straining.

5 You can reduce the broth further by simmering down with the lid removed from the pot, if a richer sauce is desired, or chill in the fridge for 2–3 days or in the freezer for 1 month.

Make a quick Thai seafood soup by crushing a lemongrass stalk in a pan of simmering shellfish broth. Simmer gently for 5 minutes, then discard the stalk. Add some fresh or dried kaffir lime leaves, shredded chilli, nam pla (Thai fish sauce) and peeled raw prawns (shrimp). Simmer gently for 3–4 minutes until the prawns (shrimp) turn pink, then stir in some shredded spring onions (scallions), chilli and chopped coriander (cilantro) or Thai basil.

Now try this...

- Shellfish broth can be made into many classic sauces and soups, such as chowders and lobster or shrimp bisque, as well as seafood stews, gumbo and risotto. It can also become the base for pasta sauces made with clams, mussels, shrimp, crab or lobster.

- For a Japanese-style soup, add some miso paste, spring onions (scallions), prawns (shrimp), shredded greens, oriental mushrooms and rice noodles to the simmering broth.

This delicious vegetable broth originated on a retreat that I was running for many of my regular guests. I was fortunate enough to have a whole day set aside for preparing several of the dishes. I was cooking on a large Aga range in a huge country house kitchen that could have catered for over 100 people, so I set up my broth pan into which I threw the 'tops', 'tails', skins and peelings from all the vegetables I was using. Then I simply added a few pints of water to cover everything and kept this pot simmering away all weekend, adding more tops and tails and liquid as the days passed. What transpired was delicious, highly nutritious and an obvious way to recycle what I had in front of me, rather than putting it all out to compost. If you have a relatively large family, this is worth doing – believe me!

Vegetable top and tail broth

MAKES APPROX. 1.2 LITRES/2 PINTS

Choose any 6–8 from the following as you will only be using what you have cut off the whole vegetables ready to discard or compost, and pick 2 herbs and one spice at a time:

onions, garlic and leeks, celery, endive, fennel, turnips, parsnips, swede (rutabaga), courgettes (zucchini), sweet potatoes, butternut squash, French, runner or broad (fava) beans, beetroot (beet), carrots, chard, kale or spinach

2.25 litres/4 pints water

2 tbsp apple cider or wine vinegar

coriander (cilantro) leaves, parsley, bay leaves, sage, thyme, rosemary or fennel

ginger, turmeric root, star anise, cloves, cinnamon or nutmeg

1 Place all your ingredients (scrapings, shavings, peelings, tops and tails, less-than-perfect leaves, strong spines of chard, curly kale and spinach) into a large cauldron (this is the Witches' Brew, after all!) and set onto a moderate heat on the hob (stovetop) for several hours, (or whilst you are cooking the main dishes for your day).

2 Check every hour to ensure that there is sufficient liquid and to stir the ingredients in the melting pot.

3 Turn off the heat at night and leave covered, but do not refrigerate, as the flavours will develop more if the broth is left at room temperature.

4 Strain the soup into another pot before ladling out your broth as needed, and heat to have as a hot drink, with mixed spice, or to add to relevant recipes.

NOTE

These broths will never taste the same twice, but that is their beauty – add flavourings and herbs as you wish, depending on the meals you are serving at the time.

Transform into Chinese egg drop soup by flavouring the simmering broth with soy sauce, shredded greens and sliced mushrooms. Whisk in some eggs at the end and as soon as they start to scramble and set, serve the soup.

Now try this...

- Make a Provençal pistou soup by poaching some young or baby vegetables in the broth until tender: peas, asparagus, broad (fava) beans, French beans, spinach, courgettes (zucchini), leeks and baby carrots. Add some diced juicy tomatoes and stir in fresh green pesto and chopped herbs before serving.

- Add chickpeas, preserved lemon and onion to a vegetable broth flavoured with cumin, garlic and a touch of harissa. Serve with a garnish of diced tomatoes, green and red (bell) peppers, chopped coriander (cilantro) and parsley and poached eggs.

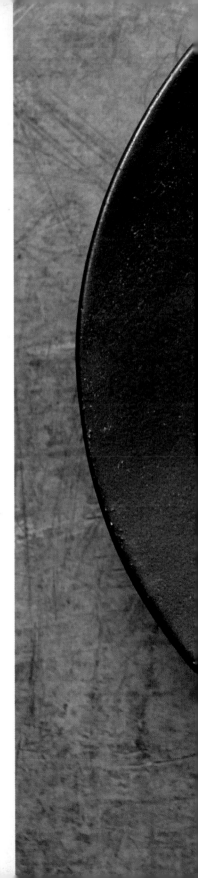

This has been adapted from the original garlic broth that many vegetarians are now cooking to enrich the flavour of pulse-based dishes. Whilst these tend to be bland in flavour until they are dressed, cooking with pulses and beans in an allium broth brings them to life immediately. The benefits of this broth are huge, as all the nutrients found in the allium family support the liver and kidneys in their detoxification processes, help to lower cholesterol and support the immune system in its constant battle against viruses and bacterial infections. Try this, and I promise it will become a favourite, even if you are a meat-eater!

Allium broth

MAKES APPROX. 1.2 LITRES/2 PINTS

2 large white onions, skin on, sliced
2 leeks, green ends included, sliced
1 bunch spring onions (scallions), sliced vertically
4–6 garlic cloves, rolled and smashed, skins on
4 small shallots, skin on, sliced into rounds
2.25 litres/4 pints water
2 tbsp white wine vinegar
4 cloves
2 bay leaves
1 tsp black peppercorns

1 Combine all the ingredients in a large pan. Cover with a lid and bring to the boil.

2 Lower the heat to a simmer, and continue cooking for 2 hours until all the allium vegetables have softened, become totally transparent and are almost reduced to a pulp.

3 Strain the broth through a sieve (strainer), pushing through the finer vegetables with a wooden spoon. Set aside to cool.

4 Store in an airtight container in the fridge for up to 5 days, or freeze for up to 3 months.

This broth is delicious if you add some diced or shredded green vegetables to it and simmer gently until they soften. Alternatively, fennel, endive and/or raddicchio all sit very well with this broth, and can be simmered gently for 10–20 minutes before adding a squeeze of lime juice, and serving straight into soup bowls for a refreshing, cleansing soup.

Now try this...

- For a cleansing detox variation that is really quick and easy to prepare, just add the following to a steaming mug of allium broth: thin slivers of garlic and fresh root ginger, some shredded greens (preferably kale, as it's a great source of potassium), a pinch each of ground turmeric and cumin, some freshly squeezed lemon or lime juice and whatever chopped herbs are handy. Delicious and so fresh-tasting and restorative.

- When you're in a hurry and need a pick-me-up, just heat up some allium broth in a pan and stir in some green pesto and lemon juice. Grind some black pepper over the top and pour into a mug.

- For a chilled soup on a warm summer's day, blitz some allium broth in a blender with the scooped-out flesh of one or two ripe avocados, some lemon juice, fresh coriander (cilantro) leaves and stalks, and a pinch of cumin or cayenne pepper. You will end up with a wonderfully velvet-textured mixture. Chill in the fridge and serve garnished with chopped coriander or chives or even some diced tomato.

SOUPS

Who can resist this classic simple soup of meltingly sweet and tender onions in a richly flavoured broth topped with floating cheesy croûtes? The secret to its success lies in the most important ingredient: the beef bone broth. A bouillon cube just won't do and will produce a pale, inferior imitation of the real thing. To serve a lighter version of this soup, you may choose to omit the cheesy croûtes and go for a healthier option, such as toasted rye cubes with a tiny sprinkling of Parmesan or Grana Padano.

French onion soup

SERVES 6

2–3 tbsp olive oil

1 knob butter

4 large onions, thinly sliced

2 tbsp plain (all-purpose) flour

1.5 litres/2½ pints boiling classic beef bone broth (see page 18)

125 ml/4 fl oz/generous ½ cup dry white wine

1 bay leaf

1 small baguette

10 ml/2 tsp Dijon mustard

125 g/4 oz/generous 1 cup grated Gruyère cheese

salt and freshly ground black pepper

1 Heat the olive oil and butter in a deep heavy-based pan over a low heat. Add the onions and cook very gently for 30–40 minutes, stirring occasionally to prevent them sticking, until they are meltingly tender and sweet and have started to caramelize and turn golden brown.

2 Stir in the flour and cook gently for 2–3 minutes, then add a little of the boiling broth, stirring until smooth and well combined.

3 Stir in the remaining broth together with the wine and bay leaf, then partially cover the pan and simmer very gently for at least 40 minutes. Season to taste with salt and pepper.

4 Preheat the grill to high. Slice the baguette into diagonal rounds and lightly toast under the grill. Thinly spread each slice with mustard.

5 Divide the soup between 6 heatproof bowls and float the toasted baguette slices, mustard-side up, on top. Sprinkle with the grated cheese and place under the hot grill for just long enough to melt the cheese. Serve immediately.

Or you can try this…

■ For an even sweeter, more intense flavour, use red onions instead of white. You can also add some fresh thyme leaves with the broth. The French use butter for cooking the onions, but olive oil is lighter and less rich.

■ The traditional cheese to use is Gruyère but Emmenthal, with its more subtle nutty flavour, also works well. If you aren't a purist and like more strongly flavoured cheese, substitute a mature Cheddar or Parmesan.

■ In France, a dash of cognac is often added to the broth while the soup is cooking to give it an even richer flavour.

There are so many recipes for chicken and vegetable soups made with Thai green curry paste but we wanted to create something more unusual. The result is this delicious, richly coloured and spicy soup made with flavourful beef bone broth. This soup is rich in alpha- and beta-carotene, which are found in the red peppers, chilli and red curry paste and are great for boosting your immune system and slowing down the aging process.

Thai red beef curry soup

SERVES 6

2 tbsp coconut oil

1 onion, thinly sliced

1 large red (bell) pepper, deseeded and thinly sliced

2 garlic cloves, sliced

2 cm/¾ in piece fresh root ginger, peeled and shredded

2 tbsp Thai red curry paste (depending on heat)

1 x 400 ml/14 fl oz can coconut milk

1 litre/1¾ pints classic beef bone broth (see page 18)

juice of 1 lime

1 tbsp nam pla (Thai fish sauce)

2 kaffir lime leaves

450 g/1 lb lean sirloin steaks (all visible fat removed)

oil, for greasing

250 g/9 oz beansprouts

4 spring onions (scallions), sliced

1 red chilli, deseeded and cut into thin strips

chopped or whole coriander (cilantro) leaves, to garnish

1 Heat the coconut oil in a large pan and cook the onion and red pepper over a low to medium heat until tender, stirring occasionally. Add the garlic and ginger and cook for 2 minutes, then stir in the curry paste and cook for 1 minute.

2 Stir in the coconut milk and then add the beef broth followed by the lime juice, nam pla and lime leaves. Simmer gently over a low heat for 15 minutes.

3 While the soup is simmering, cook the steaks in an oiled griddle pan for 2–4 minutes each side, depending on how well done you like them. Remove from the pan and cut into thin slices. Add the beansprouts to the soup and cook for 2 minutes.

4 Ladle the hot soup into 6 shallow bowls and arrange the steak strips, spring onions (scallions), chilli and coriander (cilantro) on top.

Or you can try this...

■ For a more substantial soup, add some soaked rice noodles (follow the directions on the packet) at the end or divide them between the bowls and ladle the soup over the top.

■ You can make a green chicken curry version with green curry paste, green (bell) peppers, fine green beans, mangetout (snow peas) or pak choi (bok choy), chicken broth and cubed chicken breast fillets. Fry the chicken with the onion before stirring in the curry paste and adding the broth.

■ Or you can experiment with a delicious seafood version, using green Thai curry paste and fish or shellfish broth plus a selection of fish and shellfish. Choose from firm white fish fillets, prawns (shrimp), queen scallops and baby squid. If you can't get hold of fresh fish, always keep some packs of frozen seafood (fruits de mer) in your freezer.

! Thai curry paste varies enormously in depth of heat from one manufacturer to another, so go easy on how much you add to soups and curries. Add one tablespoon at a time and taste after each addition until you achieve the required degree of heat.

Japanese food has exploded in popularity in recent years. With its clean, fresh flavours and healthy cooking methods, it is now one of the world's most widely eaten cuisines. Clear broths enriched with miso, a traditional paste made from fermented soybeans and rice or wheat, are often eaten for breakfast as well as lunch or supper. Just add a spoonful of miso to some hot bone broth for an intensely flavoured uplift during the day, or stir into marinades, soups and casseroles.

Miso ramen with beef

SERVES 4

250 g/9 oz ramen noodles

1 tbsp sesame oil (or toasted sesame oil)

200 g/7 oz shiitake or mixed oriental mushrooms, thinly sliced

1 carrot, cut into thin matchsticks

2.5 cm/1 in fresh root ginger, peeled and shredded

2 garlic cloves, thinly sliced

1 litre/1¾ pints classic hot beef bone broth (see page 18) or rich marrow bone broth (see page 22)

2 tbsp brown miso paste

1 tbsp soy sauce

200 g/7 oz pak choi (bok choy), trimmed and sliced

1 small bunch spring onions (scallions), thinly sliced

juice of 1 lime

450 g/1 lb rump or sirloin steak (all visible fat removed), cut into thin strips

oil, for grilling

snipped chives and coriander (cilantro) leaves, to garnish

1 Cook the noodles according to the pack instructions, then drain well and set aside.

2 Meanwhile, heat the sesame oil in a large pan over a medium heat and add the mushrooms and carrot. Cook briskly, stirring and tossing them in the oil, for about 3 minutes until tender. Stir in the ginger and garlic and cook for 1 minute more.

3 Add the hot broth and stir in the miso paste and soy sauce. Simmer gently for 2–3 minutes and stir in the pak choi (bok choy) and spring onions (scallions). Cook gently for 2 minutes – no longer or the pak choi will lose its fresh green colour. Add the lime juice.

4 While the soup is cooking, grill the steak strips in a lightly oiled griddle pan for 3–4 minutes, until well browned and cooked to your liking. Or you can stir-fry them in an oiled wok.

5 Divide the cooked noodles between 4 shallow bowls and pour over the soup. Arrange the beef strips on top and sprinkle with the chopped herbs.

Or you can try this...

- For a lighter soup, use white miso instead of brown. Keep a tub of miso paste in the fridge – it will stay fresh for several weeks. White miso is less salty than earthy red or brown miso, with a sweeter, more delicate flavour.

- This soup can be adapted to chicken – cut a chicken breast into cubes and cook with the vegetables until golden brown. Add dark chicken broth and then cook as outlined in the method above.

- You can also add trimmed mangetout (snow peas), baby spinach leaves, shredded cabbage or nori seaweed sheets, cut into strips.

- Vary the flavouring by experimenting with Tamari (a Japanese soy sauce that is gluten-free) and mirin (a sweet rice wine).

This is real comfort food and very warming on a cold day. Make sure you plan to cook it in advance as the split peas require soaking overnight. Pancetta used for soups tends to have had all the rich fat trimmed before cooking, making this a very well-balanced protein-fat-carbohydrate meal-in-a-bowl.

Green pea and ham soup

1 Put the split green peas in a large bowl and cover with 1 litre/1¾ pints cold water. Leave them to soak overnight. The following day, drain the soaked peas.

2 Heat the olive oil in a large pan and gently cook the onion over a low heat for about 10 minutes, until softened but not coloured. Add the garlic, pancetta or bacon and cook for 3–4 minutes, stirring occasionally, until the pancetta has started to brown all over.

3 Add the drained split peas and ham broth and bring to the boil. Carefully skim off any scum that forms on the surface and reduce the heat to low.

4 Strip the leaves from the sprigs of thyme and add to the pan with the bay leaves. Cover and simmer very gently for about 1 hour until the peas are soft. Stir the spinach into the soup and cook briefly for 2–3 minutes until wilted.

5 While the soup is simmering, heat the olive oil for the garnish in a frying pan or skillet and cook the red onion over a low heat, stirring frequently, until tender and starting to crisp and caramelize. Set aside

6 Blitz the soup in a blender (or use a stick blender) until smooth. Return to the pan and reheat very gently. Season to taste with black pepper – it probably won't need any salt as the pancetta and broth will make it sufficiently salty.

7 Ladle the soup into 6 bowls and serve topped with the caramelized onions, mint leaves and a swirl of crème fraîche.

Or you can try this...

■ The green split peas and spinach give this soup a lovely fresh green colour but, for a more earthy version, you can use yellow split peas instead.

■ If you have a cooked ham hock or ham bone, add it to the soup while it's cooking for a more intense flavour. Remove and strip the meat off the bone and dice finely before blending with the soup.

■ If you have some frozen peas in the freezer, you can add some of these to the soup about 10 minutes before the end of the cooking time.

Chicken, noodles and spices are a recurring theme in the soups of Thailand, China, Vietnam and Malaysia. Nutritionally, this is a complete meal-in-a-bowl as well as being a superb gluten-free option with the rice noodles, rather than egg noodles, which are always made from wheat.

Velvety Thai chicken noodle soup

SERVES 4

2 green chillies
2 garlic cloves, peeled
2 lemongrass stalks, peeled and chopped
1 bunch coriander (cilantro)
1 bunch Thai basil
grated zest of 1 lime
150 g/5 oz rice noodles (dried weight)
2 tbsp groundnut (peanut) or coconut oil
4 spring onions (scallions), thickly sliced
½ tsp grated fresh ginger
4 skinned, boned chicken breasts, thickly sliced
900 ml/1½ pints hot light chicken broth (see page 30)
1 x 400 ml/14 fl oz can coconut milk
1 tbsp nam pla (Thai fish sauce)
2 kaffir lime leaves, finely shredded
juice of 1 lime
fresh coriander (cilantro) leaves, to garnish
lime wedges to serve

(ILLUSTRATED ON PAGES 68–69)

1 Put the chillies, garlic, lemongrass, coriander (cilantro), basil and lime zest in a food processor or blender and blitz to a thick green paste.

2 Put the rice noodles in a large, shallow heatproof bowl and cover with boiling water. Set aside to soak for 10 minutes, stirring occasionally to prevent them sticking together.

3 Meanwhile, heat the oil in a large pan and fry the spring onions (scallions) and ginger for 1 minute. Add the chicken and stir-fry over a medium heat for about 5 minutes until golden brown.

4 Stir in the green paste and cook for 1 minute, then add the hot chicken broth, coconut milk, nam pla and kaffir lime leaves. Simmer for 5 minutes, or until the chicken is cooked through, then stir in the lime juice.

5 Drain the rice noodles and divide between 4 shallow serving bowls. Ladle the hot soup over the top, distributing the chicken slices evenly. Serve garnished with coriander (cilantro) leaves with lime wedges.

Or you can try this...

- Use 400 g/14 oz fresh rice noodles instead of dried – they don't need soaking and can be added to the soup for the last couple of minutes to heat through.

- Experiment with different herbs. Thai mint can be substituted for Thai basil and gives the soup a more subtle flavour. Don't worry if you can't get hold of Thai basil – use the ordinary kind instead.

- You can grill the chicken breasts in a griddle pan until cooked through and golden brown before slicing and adding them to the soup and noodles. Arrange them on top with a sprinkling of coriander (cilantro).

- For a richer, creamier soup, use coconut cream rather than milk, and stir it into the hot chicken broth.

Country folk have been making soup like this with game and lentils since time immemorial. Rustic and earthy, this simple dish connects you to the land and nature. It's a robust and filling dish that deserves to be accompanied by a quality artisan bread which will make it a meal in itself.

Pheasant, lentil and cabbage soup

SERVES 4

30 g/1 oz butter
4 tbsp olive oil
1 x 900 g/2 lb oven-ready pheasant
1 onion, chopped
2 sticks celery, chopped
½ bulb fennel, trimmed and finely sliced
4 spring onions (scallions), sliced
100 g/3½ oz/scant ½ cup Puy lentils
4 juniper berries
1 bouquet garni (bay leaf, sprigs of thyme and parsley)
1 litre/1¾ pints game broth (see page 39)
1 small Savoy cabbage, shredded
salt and freshly ground black pepper
1 small handful of parsley, chopped
crusty bread, to serve

(ILLUSTRATED ON PAGES 72–73)

1 Preheat the oven to 200°C/400°F/gas mark 6.

2 Heat the butter and 1 tablespoon olive oil in a roasting pan on top of the hob (stovetop) until foaming, then add the pheasant. Cook for a few minutes on each side until browned all over. Transfer the pan to the oven and roast for 30 minutes, or until the pheasant is cooked through. Remove from the oven, cover with kitchen foil and set aside to rest and cool a little.

3 Meanwhile, heat the remaining olive oil in a large pan and add the onion, celery and fennel. Cook over a low heat, stirring occasionally, until tender. Add the spring onions (scallions) and lentils and cook for 1 minute. Add the juniper berries, bouquet garni and game broth and bring to the boil. Reduce the heat and simmer gently for about 30 minutes, until the lentils are cooked but not too soft.

4 Add the cabbage and cook gently for 10 minutes – do not overcook. You want the cabbage to retain its fresh green colour.

5 Meanwhile, strip the pheasant meat off the carcass, discarding the skin (keep the carcass and use it to make another batch of game broth). Cut the meat into smallish pieces and add them to the soup. Season to taste and simmer for a few more minutes.

6 Remove the bouquet garni and ladle the soup into bowls. Sprinkle with parsley and serve with crusty bread.

Or you can try this…

- Pearl barley is a delicious alternative to lentils in this comforting soup. It adds texture and a nutty flavour as well as slightly thickening the broth.

- Other seasonal game birds, such as partridges, can be used in this way to make a winter soup.

- Spring greens, curly kale or cavolo nero, a loose-leafed, slightly bitter Italian cabbage, can be substituted for the Savoy cabbage. Experiment with whatever is plentiful and available. You could even try red onion and red cabbage.

Variations on psarosoupa – a basic soup of fish, boiled vegetables and potatoes – are served throughout Greece and its Aegean archipelago of islands. It's usually made with the fresh catch of the day – whatever fish is available – so for the best flavour use the freshest, best-quality fish you can find. There are no strict rules and, like most Greek family dishes, recipes are passed down through generations and tweaked according to preference and local and seasonal ingredients.

Aegean fish soup

SERVES 6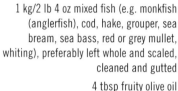

1 kg/2 lb 4 oz mixed fish (e.g. monkfish (anglerfish), cod, hake, grouper, sea bream, sea bass, red or grey mullet, whiting), preferably left whole and scaled, cleaned and gutted

4 tbsp fruity olive oil

1 large onion, chopped

1 leek, trimmed and thinly sliced

2 carrots, cut into chunks

2 sticks celery, sliced

3 garlic cloves, crushed

2 courgettes (zucchini), sliced or cut into matchsticks

500 g/1 lb 2oz potatoes, peeled and cubed

450 g/1 lb juicy tomatoes, roughly chopped

a pinch of crushed chilli flakes (optional)

1.2 litres/2 pints white fish bone broth (see page 43)

a pinch of saffron threads

3 bay leaves

2 strips orange zest

juice of 1 orange or lemon

1 small bunch flat-leaf parsley, chopped

1 small bunch dill, chopped

extra-virgin olive oil, to garnish

salt and freshly ground black pepper

1 Rinse the fish under cold running water. Pat dry with kitchen paper and cut each one through the bone into several thick pieces. Set aside.

2 Heat the olive oil in a large pan and cook the onion, leek, carrots, celery and garlic over a low heat for about 10 minutes, stirring occasionally, until softened but not not coloured.

3 Stir in the courgettes (zucchini), potatoes and tomatoes with a pinch of chilli (if using). Heat through gently and then add the fish broth, saffron, bay leaves and orange zest.

4 Bring to the boil, then reduce the heat to a very gentle simmer and cover the pan. Cook gently for 15–20 minutes until the vegetables are tender, then add the fish and simmer for a further 10–15 minutes until it is thoroughly cooked, opaque and starting to come away from the bone. Add the orange or lemon juice and season to taste.

5 Stir in the chopped herbs and ladle the soup into shallow bowls, dividing the fish equally between them. Drizzle with a little olive oil and serve.

Or you can try this...

■ To make this soup even more substantial, you can add lobster, shrimp, squid or mussels – whatever seafood is in season and readily available.

■ If you don't want to fiddle about with bones, tails, fins and skin, use fish fillets instead. You can ask the fishmonger to prepare the fish for you.

■ To enhance the flavour, a glass of white wine could be added to the simmering soup. Alternatively, a thinly sliced fennel bulb will infuse it with a subtle aniseed flavour.

■ Some Greek cooks use fewer potatoes (or omit them altogether) and add a cupful of rice to the soup 15 minutes before the end, or serve the soup poured over a toasted slice of bread sitting in the base of each bowl.

Variations on this creamy fish soup are found in all the Scandinavian countries but the two common ingredients to them all are salmon and dill. This is very filling and more of a complete meal than a first course, especially when mopped up with some rye or crusty bread. Wild salmon is undoubtedly one of the richest sources of omega-3 essential fatty acids, and it has a better flavour than the farmed sort.

Laxsoppa (Swedish fish soup)

SERVES 6

30 g/1 oz butter

1 large onion, chopped

2 leeks, trimmed and shredded

1 kg/ 2lb 4 oz waxy potatoes, peeled and cut into chunks

1 litre/1¾ pints white fish bone broth (see page 43)

2 bay leaves

2 ripe tomatoes, chopped

500 g/1 lb 2 oz salmon fillet, skinned and thickly sliced

80 g/3 oz baby spinach leaves

100 ml/3½ fl oz soured cream or crème fraîche

1 small bunch dill, chopped, and a few sprigs reserved to garnish

salt and freshly ground black pepper

rye bread, to serve

1 Melt the butter in a large pan and cook the onion and leeks over a low to medium heat, stirring occasionally until they are tender but not coloured. Add the potatoes and cook, stirring, for 8–10 minutes. Reduce the heat if the onion starts to brown.

2 Add the fish broth and bay leaves and bring to the boil. Reduce the heat and add the tomatoes. Simmer gently, partially covered, for a few minutes until the potatoes are cooked and tender.

3 Add the salmon and spinach and continue cooking gently for 5 minutes until the salmon is cooked through. Season to taste.

4 Gently stir in the soured cream or crème fraîche and chopped dill, taking care not to break the salmon slices.

5 Serve the soup in shallow bowls, garnished with sprigs of dill, with sliced rye bread.

Or you can try this...

■ In Sweden and Finland, other vegetables, usually roots such as carrots and swede (rutabaga), are sometimes added to this soup.

■ We like the acidity of soured cream or crème fraîche but if you prefer a creamier texture and richer flavour you can substitute double (heavy) cream and add a dash of lemon juice.

■ The quality of the salmon will affect the flavour of the soup. If you can find it, wild salmon is better – nutritionally and taste-wise – than the farmed sort.

For the best flavour, you need really juicy, fragrant sun-ripened tomatoes, preferably home-grown – most supermarket varieties won't make the grade and you might be better off investigating the stalls at your local farmers' markets in late and early autumn. Always be sure to sniff the tomatoes before buying; they should have a distinctively sweet scent, one of the great aromas of summer.

Roasted tomato soup with basil oil

SERVES 6

1 kg/2lb 4 oz juicy ripe tomatoes, halved
2 red onions, sliced
3 garlic cloves, unpeeled
2 carrots, sliced
a pinch of sugar
3 tbsp olive oil
900 ml/1½ pints vegetable top and tail (see page 50) or light chicken broth (see page 30)
2–3 drops balsamic vinegar
salt and freshly ground black pepper

To serve:
4 tsp crème fraîche
4 tsp basil oil
4 sprigs basil
focaccia or sourdough bread, to serve

1 Preheat the oven to 190°C/375°F/gas mark 5.

2 Place the tomatoes, cut-side up, in a roasting pan with the red onions, garlic and carrots. Sprinkle over the sugar and drizzle with the olive oil. Season with a little salt and pepper. Roast for about 45–50 minutes, until the vegetables are tender and just starting to char around the edges. Check occasionally and turn the onions and carrots in the oil to prevent them sticking.

3 Remove the garlic cloves and squeeze out the garlic, discarding the skins. Place in a pan with the roasted vegetables and broth. Bring to the boil, then reduce the heat to medium and cook for 5–10 minutes.

4 Transfer the soup to a blender or food processor and blitz, in batches, until smooth – or use a stick blender off the heat. Check the seasoning, add the balsamic vinegar and reheat the soup over a gentle heat.

5 Ladle the hot soup into bowls and swirl in the crème fraîche and basil oil. Top each bowl with a sprig of basil and serve with hunks of bread.

Or you can try this...

■ For a bright fiery red colour, substitute 2 red (bell) peppers (stalks, ribs and seeds removed) for the carrots and roast as above.

■ If you prefer a creamier texture, stir a couple of tablespoons of crème fraîche into the soup before ladling it into the bowls.

■ Don't worry if you don't have any balsamic vinegar – use red wine vinegar instead. Go easy on the balsamic as it is strongly flavoured and if you add too much it can darken the soup and destroy the vibrant, fresh colour.

In Tuscany this is made with dried beans but we've used canned ones to make it simpler – for the more traditional version see the variations below. This soup is so mineral-rich that you could make it every week just to give your immune, heart and regenerating systems a great boost. It's also an excellent source of vegetarian protein.

Tuscan bean and vegetable soup with Parmesan crisps

SERVES 4

3 tbsp olive oil

1 onion, chopped

1 leek, trimmed and chopped

2 sticks celery, chopped

2 carrots, diced

2 garlic cloves, crushed

800 ml/1 pint 7 fl oz vegetable top and tail (see page 50) or allium broth (see page 55)

450 g/1 lb ripe tomatoes, chopped (or 1 x 400 g/14 oz can)

2 potatoes, cubed

stripped leaves of 2 sprigs thyme

stripped and chopped leaves of 1 sprig rosemary

1 x 400 g/14 oz can borlotti or cannellini beans, rinsed and drained

175 g/6 oz curly kale, centre ribs and stems removed, leaves shredded

salt and freshly ground black pepper

For the Parmesan crisps:

100 g/3½ oz Parmesan, grated

1 Heat the olive oil in a large pan and cook the onion, leek, celery and carrots over a low heat for about 10 minutes, until softened but not coloured. Stir occasionally to prevent them sticking. Stir in the garlic and cook for 1 minute more.

2 Add the broth, tomatoes and potatoes and bring to the boil. Reduce the heat and add the herbs. Simmer gently for 45 minutes, until all the vegetables are cooked and tender.

3 Add the beans and kale and continue cooking for 5 minutes – be careful not to overcook the kale or it will become soggy and lose its bright green colour. Season to taste.

4 While the soup is cooking, make the Parmesan crisps. Preheat the oven to 180°C/350°F/gas mark 4 and line a baking sheet with greaseproof (parchment) paper. Add 4 circular heaps of grated Parmesan and bake for 5 minutes or until the cheese has melted and spread to form circles – don't let it get too brown. Remove from the oven and set aside to cool.

5 Ladle the soup into shallow bowls and serve with the Parmesan crisps.

Or you can try this...

■ Instead of using canned beans, which are quick and convenient, you could make the soup in the traditional way with dried beans. Soak them overnight, then rinse and drain before adding to the soup with the broth. Simmer for at least 1¼ hours, until the beans are cooked and tender, then add the kale at the end.

■ The beauty of this dish is that it's infinitely versatile and you can add almost any seasonal vegetables – courgettes (zucchini), fennel bulb, chard, spinach and cabbage all add to the flavour and nutritional benefits. For a more substantial dish, add a handful of macaroni or vermicelli about 10 minutes before the end of cooking.

■ In spring and summer, try using basil instead of rosemary with fresh new season shelled peas, broad (fava) beans, courgettes (zucchini), asparagus and fine green beans plus baby spinach leaves instead of kale. Delicious!

This is a delicious spicy soup to eat in the autumn when pumpkin is in season, especially around Hallowe'en, when it's great for using up the flesh that's scooped out from making grinning jack-o'-lanterns. Pumpkin is a good source of beta-carotene, as are most gourds and squashes. Butterbeans (lima beans) are one of the richest sources of vegetarian protein, as well as abundant zinc for healing and repair.

Pumpkin and butterbean soup with tarka

SERVES 4

2 tbsp coconut oil

1 onion, chopped

900 g/2 lb pumpkin, peeled, deseeded and cut into cubes

1 tbsp chopped fresh root ginger

1 tsp ground cumin

1 tsp ground turmeric

2 tsp coriander seeds, roasted and crushed

1.2 litres/2 pints hot vegetable top and tail broth (see page 50)

1 x 400 g/14 oz can butterbeans (lima beans), rinsed and drained

salt and freshly ground black pepper

6 tbsp low-fat natural yogurt

shredded coriander (cilantro) leaves, to serve

For the tarka topping:

2 tbsp rapeseed oil

1 small onion, thinly sliced

2 garlic cloves, thinly sliced

1 red chilli, deseeded and shredded

1 tsp yellow mustard seeds

1 tsp cumin seeds

1 Heat the coconut oil in a large pan and cook the onion over a low heat, stirring occasionally, until tender but not coloured. Add the pumpkin and cook gently, stirring it in the oil, for 3–4 minutes until golden. Add the spices and cook for 1 minute, stirring well.

2 Add the hot vegetable broth and bring to the boil. Reduce the heat, cover the pan and simmer gently for 20 minutes until the pumpkin is tender. Add the beans and heat through for a couple of minutes.

3 While the soup is cooking, make the tarka topping. Heat the oil in a frying pan over a medium heat and add the onion. Cook, stirring frequently, until it is tender, crisp and golden brown. Turn up the heat and stir in the garlic, chilli and seeds, and cook for 1 minute, or until the mustard seeds start popping. Remove from the heat – don't overcook them or the garlic will colour and taste bitter.

4 Blitz the soup to a smooth purée in a blender or food processor, or use a stick blender. Season to taste and reheat gently, then ladle into wide bowls.

Swirl a spoonful of yogurt into each portion and add the tarka topping. Scatter some coriander (cilantro) over the top and serve.

Or you can try this...

■ This soup works equally well with butternut squash or even root vegetables, such as parsnips, swede (rutabaga) and carrots, instead of pumpkin. You will still end up with a sweet, spicy flavour and a lovely deep golden-orange colour.

■ For a hotter, spicier version, try adding some dried or chopped fresh chilli or a spoonful of garam masala when cooking the onion and pumpkin.

■ To roast the coriander seeds, stir them in a small frying pan over a low heat for 1–2 minutes until they release their warm, spicy aroma.

This lovely bright green soup is perfect in spring and summer when spinach is plentiful and you want something fresh-tasting and light. The primary antioxidant lycopene is found in higher quantities in cooked tomatoes than raw, whilst young spinach is rich in iron, magnesium and vitamin C.

Spinach soup with slow-dried baby plum tomatoes

SERVES 6

For the soup:

2 tbsp olive oil

1 large onion, chopped

1 large potato, peeled and diced

1 litre/1¾ pints vegetable top and tail (see page 50) or allium broth (see page 55)

2 sprigs fresh thyme, leaves stripped

1 sprig fresh rosemary

200 g/7 oz frozen peas

1 kg/2 lb 4oz spinach leaves, chopped with any tough stalks removed

a good pinch of freshly grated nutmeg

a squeeze of lemon juice

4–5 tbsp reduced-fat crème fraîche (optional)

rosemary-infused olive oil, to drizzle (optional)

salt and freshly ground black pepper

For the slow-dried baby plum tomatoes:

2 tbsp fruity green olive oil

a few drops of balsamic vinegar

1 sprig fresh rosemary

4 sprigs fresh thyme

12 baby plum tomatoes, halved

sea salt

1 Preheat the oven to 150°C/300°F/gas mark 2.

2 To make the tomato garnish, mix together the olive oil, balsamic vinegar and herbs. Pour onto a baking sheet and add the tomatoes, turning them in the oil. Lay the tomatoes on the sheet, cut-side down, and season lightly with sea salt. Cook in the preheated oven for at least 1 hour, checking them occasionally to ensure they don't brown or burn. When cooked, they should be quite soft and starting to shrivel and wrinkle, with a concentrated sweet flavour. Remove from the oven and set aside to cool.

3 Meanwhile, make the soup. Heat the oil in a large pan and cook the onion and potato over a low heat until tender. Add the broth and bring to the boil, then turn down the heat to a simmer, add the herbs and cook gently for 15–20 minutes.

4 Stir in the peas and spinach and cook for 2–3 minutes until just tender but still a vibrant green.

5 Remove the sprig of rosemary, transfer the soup to a blender or food processor and blitz, in batches, until smooth – or use a stick blender off the heat. Return to the pan and season with nutmeg, lemon juice, salt and pepper. For a creamier consistency, stir in the crème fraîche.

6 Ladle the soup into bowls and serve garnished with the slow-dried tomatoes and a drizzle of rosemary-infused olive oil.

Or you can try this…

■ Instead of thyme and rosemary, try using mint, basil or coriander (cilantro) to flavour the soup.

■ For a richer and more flavoursome version, just stir some grated Parmesan, mature Cheddar or crumbled blue cheese into the puréed mixture and then reheat very gently until the cheese melts into the soup.

■ In springtime, substitute a handful of seasonal fresh sorrel leaves for some of the spinach. It will give the soup a lovely fresh lemony taste. You can enhance this with a squeeze of lemon juice. If you can't buy sorrel, grow a patch in your garden or plant some in a large tub on your patio.

This vibrantly coloured soup is so quick and easy to make … and it tastes as good as it looks. Beetroot (beets) are revered for their rich iron and beta-carotene content. They are vital for supporting immunity as well as having great skin-renewal properties.

Beetroot soup with horseradish cream

SERVES 6

For the soup:
2 tbsp olive oil
1 onion, chopped
1 large parsnip, diced
1 tsp fennel seeds
750 ml/1¼ pints vegetable top and tail broth (see page 50)
4 fresh raw beetroot (beets) (about 750 g/1 lb 11oz), peeled and cubed
snipped chives, to serve
salt and freshly ground black pepper

For the horseradish cream:
6 tbsp soured cream or reduced-fat crème fraîche
2 tbsp horseradish sauce

1 To make the soup, heat the olive oil in a large pan over a low heat. Add the onion, parsnip and fennel seeds and cook gently, stirring occasionally, for about 10 minutes until softened but not coloured.

2 Add the broth and bring to the boil, then reduce the heat to low and stir in the beetroot (beets). Simmer gently for 15–20 minutes until the beetroot is tender.

3 Transfer the soup to a blender or food processor and blitz, in batches, until smooth – or use a stick blender off the heat. If it's a little too thick, thin it down with some more broth. Season to taste with salt and pepper and reheat.

4 Mix together the soured cream or crème fraîche and horseradish in a bowl.

5 Ladle the soup into 6 serving bowls and swirl in the horseradish cream. Serve sprinkled with chives.

Or you can try this...

■ For a more intense beetroot (beets) flavour and a more vibrant colour, roast the beetroot first, drizzled with olive oil, at 190°C/375°F/gas mark 5 for at least an hour until tender. Add to the soup with the broth.

■ The parsnip adds sweetness to this soup but you could use a potato instead.

■ If you grow horseradish in your garden, try peeling and grating it into the cream with some grated or ground ginger for extra heat and spice.

■ Why not try something totally different with a more subtle flavour? For a sensational golden version of this soup, use yellow beets – now available in some supermarkets and from specialist stores and farmers' markets. Or buy a packet of seeds and grow your own. They are delicious plain boiled and skinned, then sliced and dressed with a lemony vinaigrette and some snipped fresh herbs.

There's no point making this delicious broth in the autumn or winter months when you have to rely on imported vegetables – it won't taste the same. You need the freshest and most intensely flavoured new season's vegetables as the hours of daylight grow longer and they start appearing in farmers' markets and your local stores. If you have a garden or allotment and grow your own, so much the better.

Spring vegetable salad broth

SERVES 4

250 g/9 oz shelled broad (fava) beans
1 Cos (Romaine) lettuce
3 tbsp olive oil
4 shallots, chopped
2 garlic cloves, thinly sliced
125 g/4 oz Chantenay baby carrots, trimmed
250 g/9 oz baby new potatoes, scrubbed and halved
1 litre/1¾ pints allium (see page 55) or vegetable top and tail broth (see page 50)
125 g/4 oz thin asparagus spears, cut into shorter lengths
100 g/3½ oz fresh podded peas
1 small bunch mint, roughly chopped
salt and freshly ground black pepper
4 tsp green pesto

1 Tip the broad (fava) beans into a pan of boiling water and cook for 1 minute. Drain immediately, then refresh under cold running water. When the beans are cool enough to handle, slip off the skins. Set aside.

2 Cut the lettuce through the centre lengthways and then cut each half through the middle again, so you end up with four quarters, each with a core. Plunge the lettuce into a pan of boiling salted water for 1½ minutes before removing with a slotted spoon and refreshing in a large bowl of cold water. Remove and pat dry with kitchen paper, then cut out and discard the central core.

3 Heat the olive oil in a large pan and cook the shallots, garlic and carrots over a low heat for about 5 minutes. Stir in the potatoes and cook for 5 more minutes.

4 Add the broth and bring to the boil. Reduce the heat and simmer gently for 10 minutes. Stir in the asparagus, peas and broad beans and simmer for 5 minutes or until all the vegetables are cooked and tender.

5 Add the lettuce leaves and mint and cook for 1 minute more. Check the seasoning and divide between 4 shallow bowls. Cool a little and serve warm with a spoonful of pesto.

Or you can try this...

■ This soup is akin to a liquid salad. If you like a sharper, more piquant taste, reminiscent of vinaigrette dressing, add a dash of lemon juice or wine vinegar or even some baby cocktail onions.

■ You can add virtually any green spring vegetables – have fun with sorrel, spinach, shredded spring greens, baby courgettes (zucchini), spring onions (scallions), small leeks or purple sprouting broccoli.

STEWS, SAUTÉS AND CASSEROLES

Sweet rust-red paprika is the spice that defines Hungarian cooking and nowhere is it put to better use than in gulyas, the national dish. With its characteristic smoky flavour, it adds colour and a subtle hint of smokiness to a range of soups, stews and casseroles made with beef, pork, sausages, bacon, potatoes, cabbage, peppers and mushrooms – the staples of a land-locked country with long, bitterly cold winters. Goulash was traditionally made with meat that had been dried in the sun and then cooked in an iron pot over an open fire.

Gulyas

SERVES 4

2 tbsp dripping or olive oil

2 red onions, thickly sliced

1 hot red chilli, deseeded and chopped (optional)

1 large red (bell) pepper, deseeded and thinly sliced

1 large green (bell) pepper, deseeded and thinly sliced

500 g/1 lb 2oz lean chuck steak or shin of beef, cubed

1 heaped tbsp plain (all-purpose) flour

2–3 tbsp Hungarian sweet paprika

2 tsp caraway seeds

400 ml/14 fl oz classic beef broth (see page 18) or rich marrow bone broth (see page 22)

1 x 400 g/14 oz can chopped tomatoes

2 tbsp red wine vinegar

125 ml/4 fl oz soured cream

salt and freshly ground black pepper

zest of 1 lemon, to garnish

2 tbsp chopped flat-leaf parsley

a good pinch of paprika to sprinkle

wide noodles, to serve

1 Preheat the oven to 140°C/275°F/gas mark 1.

2 Heat the dripping or oil in a large heavy flameproof casserole and cook the onions over a low heat for at least 10 minutes until soft. Stir them occasionally to prevent them sticking to the pan. Stir in the chilli and peppers and cook for 4–5 minutes. Remove the vegetables from the pan and set aside.

3 While the vegetables are cooking, sprinkle the beef with the flour, paprika and some salt and pepper. Stir or toss together in a bowl until the beef is well coated.

4 Add the beef to the pan and sear over a medium heat, stirring, until coloured all over. Return the cooked vegetables to the pan and stir in the caraway seeds.

5 Add the beef broth, tomatoes and red wine vinegar and heat until it starts to bubble gently and simmer. Cover the casserole and place it in the oven for 1½–2 hours, until the beef is meltingly tender and the liquid has reduced. Check the seasoning.

6 Briefly stir the soured cream into the goulash in a quick single swirl. Sprinkle the lemon zest, parsley and paprika over the top, and serve with a pile of steaming buttered noodles and some tender green cabbage.

Or you can try this...

■ Instead of beef, use lean leg or shoulder of pork, cut into cubes. In Hungary, pork is often substituted for beef.

■ If you wish, you can add mushrooms, garlic or some spicy sausage, or fresh tomatoes instead of canned ones. For a more intense flavour, add a tablespoon of tomato purée (paste) with the broth.

■ The traditional accompaniments, if not using noodles, are boiled potatoes and cabbage. Add a little butter or soured cream, some caraway seeds and a good grinding of black pepper to the cabbage, which should be cooked al dente.

In Greece, stifado is often made with rabbit or veal rather than beef. It is slow-cooked on top of the stove until the meat is so tender that it is literally falling apart, or left in a cool oven until the wine and broth reduce to a thick, glossy sauce. Keep the lid on tightly while it's cooking to keep the stew moist and prevent it drying out. Like most things Greek, you cannot rush this…the slower the better. Stifado is eaten all the year round, not just in winter, and it's a permanent fixture on the menu of most tavernas, no matter how hot it is.

Stifado

SERVES 4

4 tbsp fruity olive oil

600 g/1 lb 5 oz baby shallots, peeled

1 kg/2 lb lean stewing beef or chuck steak, cubed

3 garlic cloves, halved

125 ml/4 fl oz/generous ½ cup red wine

500 ml/18 fl oz hot classic beef bone broth (see page 18)

3 tbsp red wine vinegar

3 ripe tomatoes, chopped

1 tbsp tomato purée (paste)

1 bay leaf

2 sprigs rosemary

1 cinnamon stick

3 allspice berries

2 tbsp raisins

salt and freshly ground black pepper

orzo pasta, to serve

grated kefalotiri cheese or Parmesan, for sprinkling

1 Heat the olive oil in a large heavy pan or flameproof casserole dish and cook the shallots over a low heat for 10–15 minutes, stirring occasionally, until golden brown all over and starting to caramelize. Remove from the pan and set aside.

2 Add the beef to the pan and turn up the heat. Brown it all over and then stir in the garlic and wine. Let it bubble away and reduce for 3–4 minutes.

3 Add the broth, wine vinegar, tomatoes, tomato purée (paste), herbs and spices. Stir well, then cover the pan with a lid and simmer gently for 1 hour. Alternatively, cover the casserole, if using, and cook in a preheated oven at 140°C/275°F/gas mark 1.

4 Add the raisins and shallots to the stifado and continue cooking for about 45–60 minutes until the meat is really tender and the sauce is rich and reduced. Season to taste with salt and pepper.

5 Serve the stifado with orzo pasta and grated kefalotiri cheese (or Parmesan if you can't get it).

Or you can try this…

■ Instead of beef, try rabbit or veal – if using rabbit, substitute the beef broth with earthy game broth (see page 39).

■ Instead of serving the stifado with pasta, try potatoes roasted with rosemary in olive oil. Or, in the winter, serve it with potatoes mashed to a creamy consistency with crushed garlic, olive oil and herbs.

■ In the summer and autumn, do as the Greeks do and add some halved stoned (pitted) plums or sliced quinces to the stew for a more fruity, sweet flavour.

This Milanese classic dish of 'hollow bones' is coming back into fashion and being given a makeover. Served with gloriously yellow risotto Milanese, it is not only colourful but also flavoursome and highly nutritious due to the rich marrow inside the bones, which is traditionally extracted with a tiny spoon. If you've avoided veal in the past because of justifiable ethical concerns, it's time to start enjoying it again – most good supermarkets and quality butchers now sell Freedom Food veal from sustainable farms.

Osso bucco with gremolata

SERVES 4

2 tbsp plain (all-purpose) flour

4 x 5 cm/2 in slices veal shank (excess fat removed)

30 g/1 oz butter

2 tbsp oil

1 onion, finely chopped

1 large carrot, finely diced

1 stick celery, finely diced

grated zest of 1 lemon

1 sprig sage, finely chopped

150 ml/5 fl oz/generous ½ cup dry white wine

300 g/10 oz tomatoes, skinned and chopped

300 ml/½ pint hot rich marrow bone broth (see page 22)

a squeeze of lemon juice (optional)

salt and freshly ground black pepper

risotto Milanese to serve (see page 134)

For the gremolata:

1 large garlic clove, finely chopped

1 handful of parsley, finely chopped

grated zest of 1 unwaxed lemon

1 Place the flour in a wide, shallow bowl and season with salt and pepper. Turn the veal slices in the flour and set aside.

2 Heat the butter and oil in a large deep sauté pan and add the veal. Cook briefly on both sides until browned. Remove from the pan and set aside.

3 Add the onion, carrot and celery to the pan and cook over a low heat for 8–10 minutes until softened but not coloured. Stir occasionally to stop them sticking.

4 Add the lemon zest, sage and wine and turn up the heat. Cook, stirring occasionally, until most of the wine has evaporated.

5 Stir in the tomatoes and hot broth and return the veal slices to the pan. Cover and simmer gently over a very low heat for 1 hour, then carefully turn over the veal slices to cook the other side. Continue cooking for 30–60 minutes, until the veal is really tender and the sauce has reduced. If there's a lot of liquid, remove the lid for the last 15–30 minutes. Season to taste and add a dash of lemon juice if you wish.

6 To make the gremolata, mix the ingredients together in a small bowl. Serve the osso bucco with the risotto Milanese, and sprinkle the gremolata over the top.

Or you can try this…

■ Serve the osso bucco on a mound of creamy polenta instead of risotto. You can stir some mascarpone or grated Parmesan into the polenta for a richer, more intense flavour.

■ Instead of using fresh tomatoes, you can substitute canned chopped ones or even passata but the end result will be less subtle. Some Italian chefs leave out the tomatoes altogether.

■ For a shinier, richer sauce, you can stir in a knob of butter at the end just before serving but it adds fat and calories, of course.

Oxtail has long been neglected due to its high fat content but it has a wonderfully rich flavour and responds well to slow cooking. The Chinese have always valued it as the ultimate comfort food and braise it with a variety of spices. And now it is making a big come back here, too, due not only to its high marrow content – think osso bucco (see page 96) – but also the fat is being trimmed from the tail before it's sold.

Chinese braised oxtail

SERVES 4

1.8 kg/4 lb oxtail, fat trimmed and cut through the bone into 5 cm/2 in pieces

3–4 tbsp olive oil

2 large onions, thinly sliced

3 garlic cloves, crushed

5 cm/2 in piece fresh root ginger, peeled and chopped

1 tbsp Chinese five-spice powder

900 ml/1½ pints hot rich marrow bone broth (see page 22)

4 whole star anise

2–3 tbsp dark soy sauce

2 tbsp molasses sugar

juice of 1 orange and a wide strip of orange zest

250 g/9 oz whole shiitake mushrooms, trimmed

3 spring onions (scallions), thinly sliced

salt and freshly ground black pepper

boiled rice, to serve

steamed or boiled baby pak choi (bok choy) or Chinese greens, to serve

1 Preheat the oven to 160°C/325°F/gas mark 3.

2 Season the oxtail pieces with salt and pepper. Heat the oil in a large flameproof casserole and cook the oxtail in batches, until browned all over. Remove from the pan and set aside.

3 Add the onions and cook gently over a low heat for about 10 minutes, stirring occasionally, until softened but not coloured. Add the garlic and ginger and cook for 2 minutes.

4 Stir in the five-spice powder and hot broth, then add the star anise, soy sauce, sugar, orange juice and zest. Bring to the boil and return the oxtail to the casserole.

5 Cover and cook in the oven for 1½ hours, then turn the oxtail over and return to the oven for 1 hour. Add the mushrooms, remove the lid and cook, uncovered, for 30 minutes. The dish is ready when the oxtail is tender and falling off the bone, and the sauce is reduced, rich and glossy. Check the seasoning.

6 Serve the oxtail, sprinkled with spring onions (scallions), on a bed of boiled rice with some pak choi (bok choy) or greens.

Or you can try this…

■ Beef is equally delicious cooked this way – use 1 kg/2¼ lb lean stewing or braising beef, cut into large cubes.

■ Instead of orange juice, vary the flavour with 2 tbsp tamarind paste or 1 tbsp Chinese brown bean sauce. Or you can substitute Chinese Shaoxing rice wine or dry sherry for 125 ml/4 fl oz/½ cup broth.

■ For a hotter, even more spicy take on braised oxtail, add some finely chopped fresh chilli(es) with the garlic and ginger.

The dried porcini give this simple dish its distinctive flavour and enhances the taste of the chestnut mushrooms. If mushrooms are in season, you may be able to get hold of some fresh ceps, which will transform this simple dish into something extraordinary. All edible mushrooms contain potentially life-enhancing minerals and nutrients that support the immune system and prevent all manner of viruses from taking hold.

Pork ragu with porcini and pappardelle

SERVES 4

15 g/½ oz dried porcini mushrooms
500 g/1 lb 2 oz pork fillet, trimmed and cut into thin strips
1 tbsp olive oil
1 onion, thinly sliced
250 g/9 oz chestnut mushrooms, sliced
100 ml/3½ fl oz white wine
200 ml/7 fl oz ham hock broth (see page 27)
200 ml/7 fl oz half-fat crème fraîche
grated zest of 1 unwaxed lemon
500 g/1 lb 2 oz pappardelle (dried weight)
salt and freshly ground black pepper
3 tbsp chopped parsley

1 Put the porcini in a heatproof jug or bowl and pour over some boiling water. Set aside to soak for at least 30 minutes. Drain well, reserving the soaking liquid.

2 Season the pork with salt and pepper and brown on both sides in the olive oil in a wide deep sauté pan set over a medium to high heat. Remove the pork from the pan and set aside.

3 Add the onion and sliced mushrooms to the pan and cook, stirring occasionally, until the mushrooms are golden and the onions have softened but not coloured. Add the white wine, turn up the heat and let it bubble away until reduced by at least half.

4 Return the pork to the pan and add the drained porcini. Stir into the onion and mushrooms, and then add the ham broth and a little of the reserved porcini soaking liquid.

5 Simmer for 10–15 minutes until the pork is cooked and tender and the liquid has reduced. Stir in the crème fraîche and lemon zest and heat through gently for 2 more minutes. Check the seasoning.

6 Cook the pasta in a large pan of lightly salted boiling water according to the instructions on the packet. Drain well. Divide the cooked pasta between 4 serving plates and top with the pork ragu. Sprinkle with parsley and serve.

Or you can try this...

- You can make this ragu with veal or chicken breasts instead of pork, in which case use light chicken broth (see page 30). For a piquant touch, stir in a teaspoon of wholegrain Dijon mustard just before serving.

- Chestnut mushrooms have a more interesting colour and flavour than white button mushrooms, but you can use the common or garden ones instead.

- Any broad ribbon-type pasta, such as tagliatelle or fettuccine, works well in this recipe. And, of course, you can use fresh pasta instead of dried. Follow the instructions for cooking times – it needs a fraction of the time taken to cook dried pasta.

This traditional dish, which dates back to the sixteenth century when the Spanish conquistadors arrived in South America, gets its name from the clay pot in which it was cooked – the cazuela. Corn cobs, pumpkin, potatoes, quinoa, peppers, beans, chillies and herbs were thrown into the pot along with wild game or chicken. As with all the best stews and casseroles, the success of this dish depends on the quality of the chicken broth and there's no substitute for the real thing – richly flavoured stock made from roasted chicken bones.

Chilean pork cazuela

SERVES 4

2 tbsp olive oil

500 g/1 lb 2 oz diced belly pork

1 onion, chopped

1 red (bell) pepper, deseeded and cut into strips

400 g/14 oz pumpkin or butternut squash, peeled, deseeded and cut into large chunks

8 new potatoes, halved

12 baby carrots (e.g. Chantenay), scraped and trimmed

900 ml/1½ pints ham hock broth (see page 26)

2 fresh corn cobs, shucked and cut into 2–3 pieces

125 g/4 oz thin green beans, trimmed

dash of chilli or hot pepper sauce (or serve separately)

1 small bunch coriander (cilantro), chopped

salt and freshly ground black pepper

cooked quinoa, to serve

1 Heat the olive oil in a large heavy pan and cook the pork, turning occasionally, over a medium heat until browned all over. Remove from the pan and set aside.

2 Add the onion and red (bell) pepper and cook gently over a low heat, stirring occasionally, for 6–8 minutes, until softened. Stir in the pumpkin or squash, potatoes and carrots, and cook gently, stirring, for 2–3 minutes. Return the pork to the pan.

3 Pour in the broth and simmer gently for 20 minutes until the vegetables are tender and the pork is cooked through. Add the corn and green beans and cook over a gentle heat for 10 minutes. Season to taste and add a dash of chilli or hot pepper sauce, if using. Stir in the chopped coriander (cilantro).

4 Take 4 shallow serving bowls and place a mound of quinoa in each one. Ladle the cazuela over the top, dividing the pork and vegetables equally among them.

Or you can try this...

■ The traditional way of serving cazuela is to ladle it over some cooked quinoa in a bowl but nowadays it is often poured over cooked rice instead. Or you can add a cupful of raw rice or quinoa to the stew with the chicken and vegetables and cook for about 15–20 minutes until just tender and al dente. This helps to thicken the stew.

■ Other vegetables are sometimes added, including peas, broad (fava) beans and shredded cabbage, curly kale or spring greens. Jalapeño chillies feature in some South American versions. Each country has its own distinctive take on the basic stew: vermicelli in Peru; sweet potato and coconut milk in parts of Latin America and the Caribbean; and fish and shellfish in Ecuador.

If you've never cooked rabbit before and feel a little squeamish about the idea of eating it, put away your qualms and be more adventurous. Rabbit is a healthy white meat with a flavour not dissimilar to that of chicken and it's now enjoying a renaissance with the new interest in wild game. Always opt for wild rabbit rather than farmed – it may be more expensive but it will have a better flavour and is more humane. Your local butcher will be a good source, and many supermarkets now sell fresh as well as frozen wild rabbit meat. There are also online companies that specialize in wild rabbit and other game meats.

Creamy rabbit with pancetta and mushrooms

SERVES 4

1 rabbit, jointed, skinned and boned, and loins and leg meat cut into chunks

1 tbsp plain (all-purpose) flour

2 tbsp olive oil

15 g/½ oz butter

1 onion, finely chopped

1 leek, trimmed and sliced

125 g/4 oz pancetta, diced

300 g/10 oz button mushrooms, halved or quartered

200 ml/7 fl oz/generous ¾ cup white wine

400 ml/14 fl oz hot dark rich chicken broth (see page 34)

2 sprigs thyme

200 ml/7 fl oz half-fat crème fraîche

1–2 tsp wholegrain Dijon mustard

salt and freshly ground black pepper

500 g/1 lb 2oz fettuccine (dried weight)

4 tbsp chopped parsley or snipped chives

(ILLUSTRATED ON PAGES 104–105)

1 Lightly flour the rabbit and season with salt and pepper. Heat the oil and butter in a large deep sauté pan and fry the rabbit, turning it occasionally, until it is golden brown all over and nearly cooked through. Remove the rabbit from the pan and set aside.

2 Add the onion, leek and pancetta to the hot pan and cook over a medium heat, stirring occasionally, until the vegetables have softened and the pancetta is golden brown all over. Add the mushroom and cook for about 3 minutes, stirring, until starting to brown.

3 Pour in the white wine, turn up the heat and boil until it has reduced to half its original volume. Stir occasionally to scrape the bottom of the pan.

4 Add the hot broth and thyme and bring back to the boil. Stir in the rabbit and cook over a medium heat for about 10–15 minutes until the sauce has thickened slightly.

5 Reduce the heat and stir in the crème fraîche and mustard. Simmer gently for 5 minutes or until the sauce is thick and creamy. Season to taste.

6 Meanwhile, cook the pasta in a large pan of lightly salted boiling water according to the instructions on the packet. Drain well and toss in a little oil or butter to coat.

7 Divide the pasta between 4 serving plates, arranging it in a neat mound on each. Ladle the creamy rabbit mixture over the top of the pasta and sprinkle with parsley or chives. Serve immediately.

Or you can try this...

■ You can ask your butcher to prepare the rabbit for you – some butchers and supermarkets now sell boned rabbit loin. This recipe works well with chicken, too. You will need 500g/1lb 2oz boned and skinned chicken breasts, cut into large chunks. Cook as opposite.

■ If you are lucky enough to be able to use wild mushrooms (ceps or morels, preferably) instead of cultivated ones, they will give this dish a more distinctive flavour. Chestnut mushrooms work well, too. You could also try soaking some dried ceps and adding these with the broth.

■ Other vegetables you can add include shallots, celery and celeriac (celery root). A pinch of ground nutmeg or some grated lemon zest will add a spicy or fresh-tasting acidic touch to the sauce.

■ Or you can omit the chopped onion and caramelize some whole peeled shallots or baby pickling (pearl) onions in a little oil and butter. Add to the dish just before serving.

■ Or you can serve the rabbit with some rice, creamy mashed potatoes or crisp golden fried bread with some redcurrant or quince jelly.

Regional variations on this rustic 'hunter's' stew of chicken, vegetables, wine and broth are to be found and savoured all over Italy. What goes into the pan often depends on what's in season and available at any given moment in time. It's a great example of healthy, local and sustainable food in action, and you can experiment in the same way. The white bean smash helps to soak up the delicious juices as well as providing protein and dietary fibre. This is a veritable nutritional feast all the year round.

Chicken cacciatore with white bean smash

SERVES 4

2 tbsp plain (all-purpose) flour
8 chicken thighs or legs, skinned
2 tbsp olive oil
15 g/½ oz butter
1 garlic bulb, unpeeled and cut in half horizontally
2 carrots, diced
a few sprigs rosemary, plus extra to garnish
100 ml/7 fl oz/scant ½ cup white wine
300 ml/½ pint light chicken broth (see page 30)
200 g/7 oz juicy tomatoes, chopped
salt and freshly ground black pepper

For the white bean smash:
3 tbsp olive oil
1 onion, finely chopped
1 sprig rosemary
2 x 400 g/14 oz cans butterbeans (lima beans), haricot or cannellini beans, rinsed and drained
grated zest of 1 lemon
salt and freshly ground black pepper

1 Place the flour in a wide, shallow bowl and season with salt and pepper. Roll the chicken in the flour and set aside. Heat the oil and butter in a large heavy pan or flameproof casserole dish and add the chicken. Cook over a medium heat, turning them as they brown. When they are golden brown on all sides, remove from the pan and set aside.

2 Add the garlic and carrots and cook for 2–3 minutes, then add the rosemary. Pour in the wine and stir well. Simmer for a few minutes until it evaporates and reduces. Return the chicken to the pan and add the broth and tomatoes. Cover with a lid and simmer gently for about 45 minutes until the chicken is cooked through and really tender and the sauce has reduced. Season to taste with salt and pepper.

3 While the chicken is cooking, make the white bean smash. Heat the olive oil in a small pan and cook the onion and rosemary gently for about 10 minutes until meltingly tender. Discard the rosemary and blitz the onion with the beans and lemon zest in a blender or food processor until you have a thick purée. Reheat in the pan and season with salt and pepper.

4 Serve the smash with the chicken in its sauce, garnished with rosemary. Squeeze the garlic out of the skin into the sauce.

Or you can try this...

■ You can use a jointed chicken, including the breasts, but the dark meat of the thighs or legs has more flavour.

■ In Italy, rabbit is often cooked in this way, too. You need a rabbit, jointed into 8 pieces. Brown in the oil and butter and then follow the recipe above. Pheasant joints work equally well.

■ For a richer-tasting result, try using a robust fruity red instead of the usual white wine. If you wish, you can marinate the chicken overnight in the wine with some herbs before cooking.

Another dish that is named after the traditional pot in which it is cooked but this time it's a conical unglazed earthenware one with a shallow bottom. It's designed to use less liquid for cooking the meat and for the steam to rise inside the lid where it condenses and the liquid descends to keep everything moist. In Morocco, the tagine is cooked over an open fire but we've adapted the recipe for the contemporary kitchen. Fresh or dried fruit is nearly always added to a tagine; apricots are a great source of beta-carotene for protecting and boosting the immune system.

Chicken, aubergine and apricot tagine

SERVES 4

2 tbsp olive oil
8 chicken thighs
2 onions, sliced
2 garlic cloves, finely chopped
1 red (bell) pepper, deseeded and sliced
1 large or 2 small aubergines (eggplant), cubed
1 tsp ground cumin
½ tsp ground ginger
1 tbsp Ras el Hanout spice mix
4 juicy tomatoes, chopped
300 ml/½ pint hot dark rich chicken broth (see page 34)
a few strands of saffron
chopped pulp and zest of 1 preserved lemon
100 g/3½ oz ready-to-eat dried apricots
1 x 400 g/14 oz can chickpeas, rinsed and drained
4 tbsp black olives
a dash of lemon juice (optional)
salt and freshly ground black pepper
1 handful of coriander (cilantro), chopped, to garnish
1 handful of flat-leaf parsley, chopped, to garnish
125 g/4 oz natural yogurt swirled with a dash of harissa paste, to serve
flatbreads and green salad, to serve

1 Heat the olive oil in a wide heavy-based pan and cook the chicken over a medium to high heat, turning it occasionally, until browned all over. Remove and set aside.

2 Add the onions and garlic to the pan and cook for about 8 minutes, stirring occasionally, until softened and starting to colour. Add the red (bell) pepper and aubergines (eggplant) and cook for a few minutes until tender.

3 Stir in the spices and cook for for 1 minute before adding the tomatoes, hot chicken broth, saffron, preserved lemon and apricots. Return the chicken to the pan and arrange on top of the vegetables. Cover the pan with a tight-fitting lid and cook gently over a low heat for 40–45 minutes until the chicken is cooked and the liquid has reduced.

4 Stir in the chickpeas and olives and check the seasoning. At this stage you can add some lemon juice if you feel that the sauce needs its sharpness. Simmer gently, uncovered, for a few more minutes.

5 Sprinkle over the coriander (cilantro) and parsley and serve with the harissa-swirled yogurt with some flatbread and salad.

Or you can try this...

■ Try serving the tagine with bulghur wheat, tabbouleh or couscous to absorb the spicy liquid. Flatbread or just a hunk of crusty bread is commonly eaten to mop up the sauce.

■ Chicken thighs have a more pronounced flavour than the white breast meat and are better than legs, too. Of course, you can joint a whole chicken and cook it in this way. In North Africa, lamb is commonly used instead of chicken. You will need about 450 g/1 lb cubed lean meat from the leg.

■ Don't fret if you can't get preserved lemons – just roughly chop a fresh one and add to the tagine.

A vegetable hotpot makes a healthy and quick and easy meal – perfect for when you get home from work and don't want to spend a long time in the kitchen slaving over a hot stove. All you need to make this are some really fresh vegetables (preferably organic), some great homemade broth, a bottle of soy sauce and a pack of rice noodles. As this hotpot proves, sometimes the simplest food tastes the best.

Asian green hotpot with rice noodles

SERVES 4

2 pak choi (bok choy), trimmed and each cut into 4 wedges lengthwise

200 g/7 oz wide rice noodles

3 tbsp groundnut (peanut) oil

1 large aubergine (eggplant), cubed

2.5 cm/1 in piece fresh root ginger, peeled and diced

1 red chilli, deseeded and shredded

2 garlic cloves, thinly sliced

400 ml/14 fl oz hot vegetable top and tail broth (see page 50) or chicken bone broth (see page 30)

2 tbsp soy sauce

a pinch of sugar

125 g/4 oz mangetout (snow peas) or sugar snap peas, trimmed

100 g/3½ oz baby spinach leaves

a handful of coriander (cilantro), chopped

1 Bring a pan of salted water to the boil and add the pak choi (bok choy). Cook for 2–3 minutes until just tender but still retaining some bite. Drain, plunge into a bowl of cold water and then drain again.

2 Put the rice noodles in a bowl and pour over some boiling water. Set aside for at least 10 minutes or follow the instructions on the packet.

3 Meanwhile, heat the oil in a large pan and cook the aubergine (eggplant) over a medium heat for about 5 minutes, turning it occasionally, until just tender and golden brown. Add the ginger, chilli and garlic to the pan and cook, stirring, for 2–3 minutes without colouring.

4 Pour in the hot broth, soy sauce and sugar and simmer for 5 minutes. Add the mangetout (snow peas) or sugar snap peas and cook gently for 3–4 minutes until just tender. Stir in the rice noodles, spinach and pak choi and cook for 2 minutes until the spinach wilts.

5 Stir in the coriander (cilantro) and ladle the hotpot into 4 shallow bowls.

Or you can try this…

■ You can add fried or griddled tofu, grilled sliced chicken or griddled steak or large prawns (shrimp) to make this hotpot more substantial and filling. Or omit the noodles and serve it spooned over a mound of boiled Thai fragrant jasmine rice.

■ It can be adapted to different Asian cuisines, depending on the flavourings you use: mirin, sake, Teriyaki or Tamari sauce for Japanese; and nam pla (Thai fish sauce), lemongrass, lime juice and green curry paste for Thai.

■ Other suitable vegetables include broccoli florets, courgettes (zucchini), Chinese cabbage, beansprouts and sliced shiitake or chestnut mushrooms.

Wild game birds are such a healthy choice – low in fat, high in protein and rich in body-building, energy-yielding nutrients with none of the additives found in much of the farmed meat and poultry many of us buy. Pheasants used to be eaten mostly by peasants as they were free food, but they are now considered a luxury item. There's not a lot of meat on a pheasant and, as a general rule, one bird will feed two.

Pot-roasted pheasants with barley

SERVES 4

4 tbsp olive oil
50 g/2 oz butter
2 oven-ready pheasants
2 parsnips, cut into chunks
1 butternut squash, peeled, deseeded and cut into chunks
1 small celeriac (celery root), cut into wedges
1 bay leaf
2 sprigs thyme
200 ml/7 fl oz Marsala
4 streaky bacon rashers
salt and freshly ground black pepper
12 shallots, peeled
2 tbsp balsamic vinegar

For the barley:
400 ml/14 fl oz game broth (see page 39)
125 g/4 oz pearl barley

1 Preheat the oven to 200°C/400°F/gas mark 6.

2 To make the barley, bring the game broth to the boil in a large pan and tip in the pearl barley. Reduce the heat, cover the pan and simmer gently for 25 minutes until the barley is just tender but still a little firm – not soft and mushy.

3 While the barley is cooking, heat 2 tablespoons olive oil and half the butter in a deep flameproof casserole. Add the pheasants, breast-side down, and cook until golden brown. Turn them over and brown them underneath and then on their sides. Remove from the pan, season with a little salt and pepper and set aside.

4 Add the parsnips, squash and celeriac (celery root) to the casserole and cook, stirring occasionally, over a low to medium heat for about 10 minutes. Add the pearl barley, game broth and herbs and pour in the Marsala. Place the pheasants on top with 2 bacon rashers covering their breasts.

5 Cover the casserole and cook in the oven for about 30 minutes. Remove the lid for the last 10 minutes to crisp up the pheasants and bacon.

6 While the pheasants are cooking, heat the remaining oil and butter in a frying pan and cook the shallots over a low to medium heat for about 15 minutes, stirring occasionally, until tender, golden brown all over and starting to caramelize. Add the balsamic vinegar and cook for 2–3 minutes. Carve the pheasants and serve on a mound of barley and vegetables with the caramelized shallots.

Or you can try this...

■ Instead of Marsala you could try Madeira or amontillado sherry or even a medium dry white wine.

■ Any root vegetables can be sautéed and then mixed into the barley, including sliced carrots and swede (rutabaga), or chopped red onion, leeks, celery, cubed sweet potatoes or quartered mushrooms.

■ A dollop of redcurrant, quince or apple herb jelly adds the perfect finishing touch to this autumnal casserole.

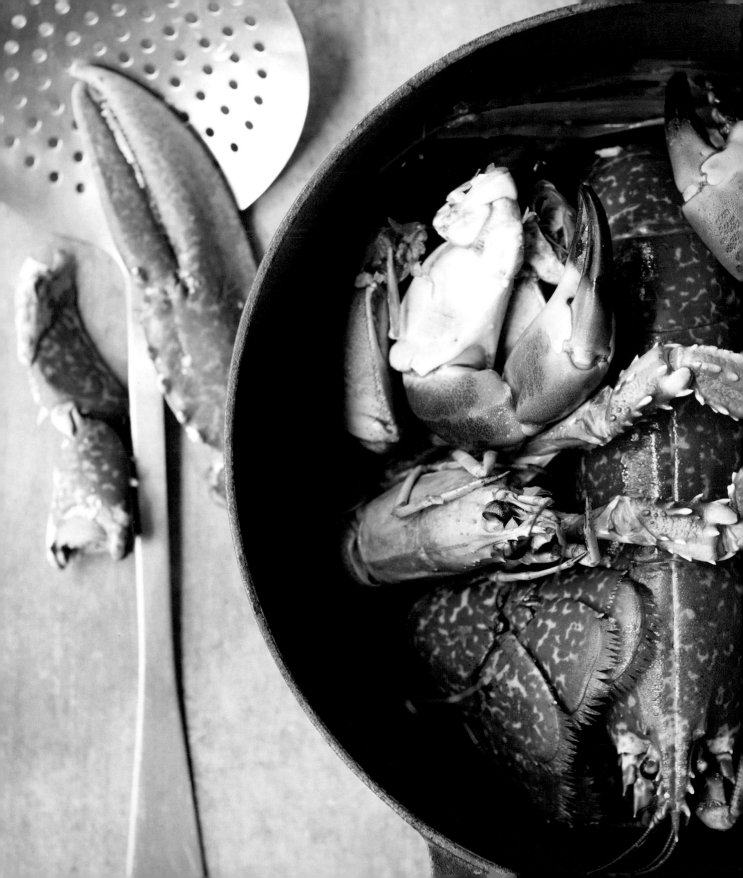

Which fish or shellfish you put into this fish stew is entirely up to you. There are no hard and fast rules. Even in Venice it often depends on which fish are available on the marble slabs in the Rialto market on any given day. The authentic versions of brodetto are made with whole fish and shellfish, giving you the tactile pleasure of picking the meat off the bones and prising it from the shells. However, if you're a bit squeamish about heads and fins or don't enjoy the messy business of eating this way, you can use filleted fish instead.

Brodetto di pesce

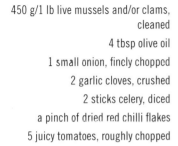

SERVES 4

450 g/1 lb live mussels and/or clams, cleaned

4 tbsp olive oil

1 small onion, finely chopped

2 garlic cloves, crushed

2 sticks celery, diced

a pinch of dried red chilli flakes

5 juicy tomatoes, roughly chopped

150 ml/¼ pint/generous ½ cup white wine

1.5 litres/2½ pints hot white fish broth (see page 43)

300 g/11 oz raw tiger prawns (jumbo shrimp) or 4 langoustines

1 kg/2 lb 4oz mixed fish, cleaned and left whole or cut into pieces, or 450 g/1 lb fish fillets, e.g. red mullet, monkfish (anglerfish), cod, whiting and grouper, cut into large chunks

salt and freshly ground black pepper

juice of 1 small lemon

1 small bunch parsley, chopped

griddled sliced focaccia or sourdough bread, to serve

(ILLUSTRATED ON PAGES 116–117)

1 Put the mussels and clams in a pan with 250 ml/8 fl oz water over a medium to high heat. Cover the pan and cook for about 4–5 minutes, giving the pan an occasional gentle shake, until the shells open. Discard any mussels and clams that don't open. When they are cool enough to handle, remove the meat from most of the shells, leaving a few in the shells for the garnish. Set aside.

2 Heat the olive oil in a deep heavy pan and cook the onion, garlic and celery over a medium heat, stirring occasionally, for about 8 minutes until tender but not coloured. Stir in the chilli flakes and tomatoes and cook for a few minutes.

3 Add the wine and cook briskly until it reduces by at least half. Stir in the fish broth and bring to a simmer. Add the prawns (jumbo shrimp) or langoustines and cook gently for a few minutes until they turn pink.

4 Gently add the fish to the pan and simmer until it is cooked through and the flesh is opaque and starting to flake. The time taken will depend on whether you are using fish on the bone – either whole or cut into pieces – or filleted chunks.

5 Season to taste with salt and pepper and add the cooked mussels and clams. Stir in the lemon juice and parsley.

6 Ladle into wide shallow serving bowls and serve immediately with grilled thick slices of bread to mop up the delicious broth.

Or you can try this...

■ Brodetto is a moveable feast and there are many variations along the Adriatic coast. Crab, baby calamari, squid, lobster, scallops and almost any firm-fleshed fish can be added, so there's no need to slavishly follow the fish and shellfish we've suggested above.

■ For a much richer-tasting brodetto, you could substitute shellfish broth (see page 47) for white fish broth. Whichever you use, it's a good idea to have it simmering ready in a pan before adding it to the vegetables.

This is such a quick and easy dinner to prepare – and it looks and tastes fabulous. Really, it's a spiced-up version of the classic French moules marinières. If you're a fan of mussels and like hot, fragrant food, you can't fail to enjoy this, plus they're healthy, meaty, high in protein and low in fat and calories.

Thai mussels with noodles

SERVES 4

2 kg/4 lb 7oz live mussels
300 g/11 oz rice noodles
1 tbsp coconut oil
3 Thai shallots, finely chopped
2 garlic cloves, crushed
1 tsp grated fresh root ginger
1 red bird's eye chilli, shredded
1 stalk lemongrass, cut into 4 pieces
1 x 400 ml/14 fl oz can coconut milk
400 ml/14 fl oz white fish bone broth (see page 43)
1 tbsp nam pla (Thai fish sauce)
2 kaffir lime leaves
juice of 1 lime
1 tsp palm sugar
1 small bunch coriander (cilantro), chopped
1 red bird's eye chilli, deseeded and shredded, to garnish

1 Prepare the mussels. Put them in a large bowl of cold water and discard any that stay open – they should all shut tightly. Pull off the little wispy beards and scrub the shells.

2 Soak the rice noodles in hot water according to the instructions on the packet.

3 Meanwhile, heat the coconut oil in a large saucepan and cook the shallots and garlic over a medium heat until the shallots are softened and golden. Stir in the ginger, chilli and lemongrass and cook for 1 minute.

4 Pour in the coconut milk, fish broth and nam pla (Thai fish sauce). Stir in the kaffir lime leaves, lime juice and sugar and turn up the heat. When it's nearly boiling, tip in the mussels.

5 Reduce the heat, cover the pan with a lid and simmer gently for 3–4 minutes, shaking the pan two or three times, until the mussels open. Remove and discard any that fail to open.

6 Stir in the drained cooked noodles and the coriander (cilantro). Divide the mixture between 4 shallow serving bowls. Scatter the shreds of chilli over the top and serve.

Or you can try this...

■ Omit the noodles and ladle the mussels in their broth over a mound of boiled fragrant jasmine rice.

■ Intensely aromatic Thai basil or mint makes an interesting change from coriander (cilantro). You can use fresh or dried kaffir lime leaves, plus a couple of shredded leaves for the garnish.

■ We've used one chilli in the stew and another to garnish the dish, but you can play around with this, depending on your personal taste. Remember that the seeds are very hot, so you can remove them, if you wish. Never ever touch your eyes or mouth when preparing chillies and always wash your hands thoroughly afterwards.

Is a laksa a soup or a main course? Whichever you decide, it's definitely a meal in a bowl, and although it looks like a long list of ingredients it's very quick and easy to make … and infinitely versatile. All you need are a food processor or blender to blitz the aromatic paste — or a pestle and mortar if you prefer an edgier, coarser paste — and a large heavy pan.

Prawn laksa with vermicelli rice noodles

SERVES 4

200 g/7 oz vermicelli rice noodles (dried weight)

1 tbsp coconut or groundnut (peanut) oil

1 x 400 ml/14 fl oz can coconut milk

500 ml white fish bone (see page 43) or shellfish broth (see page 47)

1–2 tbsp nam pla (Thai fish sauce)

juice of 1 lime

675 g/1½ lb raw peeled large prawns (jumbo shrimp), fresh or frozen and thawed

250 g/9 oz mixed mangetout (snow peas), halved lengthways, or baby spinach leaves or purple sprouting broccoli

1 handful coriander (cilantro) leaves, roughly chopped

4 spring onions (scallions), shredded

1 red chilli, deseeded and shredded

For the laksa paste:

2 red bird's eye chillies

2 stalks lemongrass, peeled and chopped

4 shallots, diced

3 garlic cloves

4 fresh kaffir lime leaves, shredded

5 cm/2 in piece fresh root ginger, peeled and chopped

2 tsp ground turmeric

1 tsp palm sugar (jaggery) or brown sugar

1 tsp shrimp paste (optional)

1 tbsp tamarind paste (optional)

1 handful coriander (cilantro) leaves, stalks and roots

1 To make the laksa paste, put everything in a food processor or blender and blitz until thick and smooth.

2 Soak the rice noodles in boiling or hot water, according to the instructions on the packet. Drain well and set aside.

3 Heat the coconut or groundnut (peanut) oil in a large pan and add the laksa paste. Stir over a low to medium heat for 2–3 minutes until it releases its aroma but do not allow to brown or burn. Add the coconut milk and broth and bring to the boil.

4 Reduce the heat to a simmer and stir in the nam pla (Thai fish sauce), lime juice and prawns (shrimp). Simmer gently for 4–5 minutes until the prawns turn pink.

5 Meanwhile, steam the vegetables of your choice or cook briefly in boiling water until just tender but still al dente with a lovely fresh green colour. Drain and add to the laksa.

6 Divide the noodles equally between 4 deep serving plates. Stir the coriander (cilantro) into the laksa and ladle over the top of the noodles. Sprinkle with the spring onions (scallions) and chilli and serve.

Or you can try this…

■ Crab claws, scallops, clams, mussels, lobster and chunks of boned, skinned monkfish (anglerfish) or cod instead of, or in addition to, the prawns (shrimp) also make a delicious seafood laksa. You could even add chunks of skinned salmon fillet with some chopped dill. Or, for a meaty alternative, try diced chicken with chicken broth and add some ground peanuts to the laksa paste.

■ The tamarind and shrimp paste are optional but try to use them if you can, particularly the tamarind, whose sourness helps offset the sweetness of the sugar and the bright zingy citrus flavour of the lime. This is very much a moveable feast: some cooks add sliced galangal, ground paprika, ground cumin, fresh mint or Thai basil to the laksa paste mixture. And the number of chillies you use depends on their heat and how much mouth-numbing fire you can tolerate.

Make this in late spring or early summer when fresh broad (fava) beans and peas are coming into season and are at their sweetest. If you can get hold of it, wild salmon is more flavoursome and less fatty than farmed. Choose the wild Alaskan sort if possible as it has fed on wild krill in the colder water of the large northern oceans. Farmed salmon can be bred in very little time and fed foods and colourings to enhance the pink flesh that develops naturally in their wild cousins.

Griddled salmon in a spring vegetable broth

SERVES 4

125 g/4 oz podded fresh broad (fava) beans

900 ml/1½ pints top and tail vegetable broth (see page 50)

1 small fennel bulb, thinly sliced plus feathery fronds

200 g/7 oz podded fresh peas

1 bunch spring onions (scallions), sliced

250 g/9 oz pak choi (bok choy), thickly sliced

a pinch of sugar (optional)

4 x 150 g/5 oz salmon fillets

salt and freshly ground black pepper

baby new potatoes (preferably Jersey Royals), to serve

For the rocket mayonnaise:

50 g/2 oz rocket leaves

2 tbsp snipped chives

2 tbsp chopped parsley or tarragon

1 tsp Dijon mustard

1 medium egg yolk

juice of ½ lemon

100 ml/3½ fl oz fruity olive oil

50 ml/2 fl oz double cream, whipped

1 Make the rocket mayonnaise. Briefly blanch the rocket in a small pan of boiling lightly salted water for a few seconds until it starts to wilt. Drain in a colander and cool under the running cold tap. Drain and gently pat dry with kitchen paper.

2 Blitz in a blender or food processor with the herbs, mustard and egg yolk. Add the lemon juice and then add the olive oil in a slow steady stream through the feed tube, while the motor is running, until the mayonnaise is thick and smooth. Transfer to a bowl and season to taste. Gently stir in the whipped cream. Cover and set aside in the fridge or a cool place.

3 Bring a small pan of water to the boil and add the podded broad (fava) beans. Cover the pan and simmer gently for about 3 minutes until the beans are tender. Drain and cool under running cold water (as above). Use your fingers to gently squeeze the green beans out of their grey outer casings.

4 Heat the vegetable broth in a large pan and bring to the boil. Reduce the heat, add the fennel bulb (reserving the fronds) and cook gently for about 5 minutes. Add the peas, spring onions (scallions) and pak choi (bok choy) and simmer for 2–3 minutes until just tender. Stir in the cooked broad beans and season to taste, adding a pinch of sugar, if you wish, to enhance the sweetness of the peas.

5 Meanwhile, cook the salmon fillets in a lightly oiled griddle pan or frying pan for 4–5 minutes each side until the salmon is opaque and cooked through and the skin is crisp and golden brown.

6 Divide the broth between 4 shallow bowls or deep plates. Place a salmon fillet on top of each one and a dollop of rocket mayonnaise. Serve immediately, garnished with the chopped feathery fennel fronds, with boiled new potatoes.

Or you can try this…

■ Halve the new potatoes and add them to the vegetable broth with the fennel. If you don't like the aniseed taste of fennel, leave it out and use some tender young asparagus spears, cut into lengths, instead.

When it's a cold night or you're in need of real comfort food, a bowl of steaming dhal never fails to warm you up. In India, dhal is not just lentils and the name encompasses all manner of pulses, dried beans and peas. The combination of lentils and sweet potatoes makes this a great sustaining dish. And, what's more, it's inexpensive, simple to prepare and cook, and tastes delicious.

Dhal with griddled sweet potato

SERVES 4

2 tbsp sunflower or groundnut (peanut) oil

2 garlic cloves, crushed

1 tsp grated fresh root ginger

1 red chilli, deseeded and finely diced

1 tsp black mustard seeds

1 tsp ground turmeric

1 tsp garam masala

250 g/9 oz split red lentils

500 ml/16 fl oz vegetable top and tail broth (see page 50)

1 x 400 ml/14 fl oz can coconut milk

4 ripe tomatoes, roughly chopped

1 large sweet potato, cut into thin wedges (skin left on)

100 g/3½ oz baby spinach leaves

juice of 1 lime

naan bread or chapatis, to serve

For the spicy onion topping:

2 tbsp sunflower or groundnut (peanut) oil

1 large onion, thinly sliced

1 tsp cumin seeds

1 red chilli, deseeded and cut into thin shreds

8 fresh curry leaves

1 Heat 1 tablespoon oil in a large heavy pan and cook the garlic, ginger and chilli over a low to medium heat for 2 minutes without colouring.

2 Stir in the mustard seeds and ground spices and when the mustard seeds start to pop, add the lentils, vegetable broth and coconut milk. Bring to the boil, then reduce the heat and simmer gently for 15 minutes. Add the tomatoes and simmer for 15 minutes until the dhal is thick and creamy in texture. If it's still a bit liquid, cook for a little longer; if it's too thick, add some more broth.

3 Make the spicy onion topping. Heat the oil in a shallow pan and cook the onion, stirring occasionally, until it starts to caramelize and turn golden brown. Add the cumin seeds, chilli and curry leaves and cook for 2 minutes. Season lightly with salt and pepper.

4 When the dhal is nearly ready, put the sweet potato with the remaining oil and some salt and pepper in a bowl and toss gently together. Heat a griddle pan until it's really hot and cook the sweet potato for 2–3 minutes each side until tender and slightly charred.

5 Stir the spinach leaves, lime juice and sweet potato into the dhal and season with salt and pepper. Spoon into 4 bowls and top each with a spoonful of the spicy onion mixture. Serve with warm naan or chapatis.

Or you can try this...

■ A fresh green coconut chutney is also a great accompaniment to dhal. It's so quick and easy to make: just blitz some grated fresh or desiccated coconut and peeled fresh root ginger in a blender with a handful each of fresh coriander (cilantro) and mint plus fresh chillies and garlic (according to taste). Add a pinch of sugar, a teaspoon of cumin or fennel seeds and some lime juice. You will end up with a delicious spicy green chutney.

■ You can vary the spices by adding cumin, fennel, cardamom or coriander seeds and ground cinnamon. If you like the citrus taste of coriander, scatter with some of the chopped leaves before adding the spicy onion topping.

This classic Roman stew of tender young green vegetables is a great way to celebrate the arrival of spring. It is so well loved that variations on the classic version are now found on trattoria menus all over Italy with locally grown vegetables and herbs added as they come into season and different cheeses, such as Pecorino or Gran Padano, and regional garnishes.

Vignole

SERVES 4

200 g/7 oz podded broad (fava) beans

3 tbsp extra virgin olive oil, plus extra for drizzling

1 onion, thinly sliced

2 garlic cloves, thinly sliced

8 baby leeks, trimmed and halved

12 young thin asparagus spears, trimmed and cut into short lengths

300 ml/½ pint vegetable top and tail broth (see page 50) or allium broth (see page 55)

200 g/7 oz podded fresh peas

4 baby artichoke hearts in oil

200 g/7 oz spinach or Swiss chard, shredded

1 small bunch mint, chopped

Parmesan cheese (Parmigiano Reggiano) shavings, to serve

1 Add the broad (fava) beans to a small pan of boiling water. Cover and simmer gently for about 3 minutes until the beans are just tender. Drain and cool under cold running water. Use your fingers to gently squeeze the green beans out of their grey outer casings. Set aside.

2 Heat the olive oil in a large pan and cook the onion and garlic over a low heat, stirring occasionally, until softened but not coloured. Add the leeks and asparagus and cook gently for about 3 minutes, turning them occasionally.

3 Pour in the vegetable broth and turn up the heat. Add the peas and when the broth is nearly boiling, reduce it to a simmer and cook for 10 minutes.

4 Add the broad beans, artichoke hearts and spinach or chard. Cook gently for 6–8 minutes until all the vegetables are tender and retain their fresh green colour. Season to taste with salt and pepper.

5 Stir in the chopped mint and serve the vignole ladled into shallow bowls with a drizzle of olive oil. Scatter with shavings of Parmesan.

Or you can try this...

■ If you can get hold of some fresh young artichokes, preferably the small ones, use these instead of the prepared ones in oil. They will enhance the overall flavour. To prepare fresh artichokes, trim the stalks to the base of the choke and remove any tough outer leaves. Cook in a pan of boiling salted water for about 10 minutes until just tender. Drain well and when cool enough to handle, gently ease back the outer leaves and remove the choke with a teaspoon. Cut in half or into quarters.

■ Other vegetables and herbs you can use include red onions or small white pickling (pearl) onions, spring onions (scallions), baby courgettes (zucchini), tender spring greens, curly or flat-leaf parsley and basil.

■ For a more substantial meal, you can stir some cooked pasta, such as tagliatelle, fettuccine or linguine, into the cooked vignole and serve sprinkled with some shredded Parmesan.

This stew can be enjoyed all year round, not just on cold winter evenings. It's peasant food at its simple best so it's worth using the best-quality ingredients you can find. Cavolo nero is a type of loose-leafed Italian cabbage which is similar to kale but has a slightly more bitter flavour. The leaves are so dark that they are nearly black (nero), and they're a great source of vitamins and minerals.

Tuscan stewed beans and cavolo nero

SERVES 4

250 g/9 oz dried beans, e.g. cannellini, butterbeans (lima beans), flageolet or borlotti beans, soaked in cold water overnight

1 bay leaf

5 tbsp fruity green olive oil, plus extra for drizzling

2 large onions, thinly sliced

2 garlic cloves, crushed

250 g/9 oz baby carrots, trimmed

a pinch of crushed red chilli flakes (pepperoncini)

600 ml/1 pint top and tail vegetable broth (see page 50) or allium broth (see page 55)

2 sprigs rosemary

a heel of Parmesan (optional)

3 ripe tomatoes, chopped

a pinch of sugar (optional)

250 g/9 oz cavolo nero, cut into wedges or roughly shredded

juice of ½ lemon

1 small loaf crusty Pugliese bread or focaccia

2 garlic cloves, halved

salt and freshly ground black pepper

sprigs rosemary, to garnish

green pesto, to serve

1 Drain the beans and place them with a bay leaf in a large pan. Cover with fresh water and bring to the boil. Remove any scum on the surface with a slotted spoon and add 2 tablespoons olive oil. Boil for about 1 hour until the beans are tender but not mushy.

2 Heat 3 tablespoons olive oil in a deep pan and cook the onions and garlic over a low to medium heat, stirring occasionally, until they soften. Add the carrots and cook gently for 3–4 minutes. Stir in the chilli flakes. Add the broth, rosemary, Parmesan (if using), tomatoes and sugar. Turn up the heat and when the broth starts to boil, turn it down to a simmer and cook gently for about 45 minutes.

3 Add the cavolo nero and simmer gently for 2–3 minutes until it wilts – not too long or it will lose its texture and colour. Add the cooked beans together with some lemon juice and seasoning to taste.

4 While the stew is cooking, preheat the oven to 180°C/350°F/gas mark 4. Cut the bread into thick slices and rub one side of each with a cut garlic clove. Place on a baking sheet, drizzle with olive oil and season lightly with salt and pepper. Bake in the preheated oven for a few minutes until toasted and golden brown.

5 Ladle the stew into wide shallow bowls, garnish with rosemary, drizzle with olive oil and add a small spoonful of pesto. Serve with the toasted bread.

Or you can try this...

■ If you don't have time to soak and cook the dried beans, leave this step out and start by frying the onions and garlic. Add two cans of rinsed, drained beans with the cavolo nero. For additional colour, why not use one can of kidney beans and one of white beans?

■ In Tuscany, cooks often fry some cubed pancetta with the onions and garlic. If you have a ham bone, this can be added with the broth to enhance the flavour.

■ Depending on the season, you can use curly kale, red kale, spring greens, spinach or even Savoy cabbage. If you wish, stir in some pungent torn basil or chopped flat-leaf parsley at the end.

RICE AND GRAINS

There are so many recipes for risotto that it's not surprising that many of us are confused as to what is the genuine article. Opinions vary widely on which rice to use, whether butter is better than oil, whether the broth should be added all at once or a ladleful at a time. However, the common ingredient in every risotto is a well-flavoured, full-bodied broth – it makes all the difference between success and a lacklustre facsimile of this delicious dish. We have included the rich beef bone marrow in our recipe but if you don't eat red meat use the dark rich chicken broth (page 34) instead.

Classic risotto Milanese

SERVES 4

85 g/3 oz unsalted butter

1 onion, finely chopped

45 g/1½ oz raw beef bone marrow, chopped (optional)

1.2 litres/2 pints rich marrow bone broth (see page 22) or dark rich chicken broth (see page 34)

250 g/9 oz/scant 1½ cups Arborio or Carnaroli risotto rice

100 ml/3½ fl oz/scant ½ cup white vermouth

1 tsp saffron threads

salt and freshly ground black pepper

50 g/2 oz fresh Parmesan, grated, plus extra for sprinkling

1 Heat half the butter in a wide heavy-based pan over a low heat and add the onion and beef marrow (if using). Cook gently for at least 10 minutes until the onion is really soft but not coloured.

2 While the onion is cooking, heat the broth in a pan and keep it simmering.

3 Add the rice to the onion and stir well until all the grains are glistening with butter and so hot they begin to crackle, but be careful not to let them colour. Pour in the vermouth cook until the liquid has almost evaporated, then add a ladleful of the simmering broth together with the saffron.

4 Be patient and keep stirring until all the liquid has been absorbed before adding another ladle of simmering broth. Keep doing this for about 20 minutes until the risotto is thick and the rice grains are plump and swollen but still slightly firm to the bite (al dente).

5 Remove the pan from the heat and stir in the remaining butter. Season to taste and stir in the Parmesan. At this point, beat the risotto with a wooden spoon until it is really glossy and creamy.

6 Cover and set aside to rest for at least 2–3 minutes before serving sprinkled with additional Parmesan if you wish.

Or you can try this…

■ Substitute a glass of good dry white wine for the vermouth – the flavour of the risotto will be a touch more subtle.

■ Some Italian chefs fold in a spoonful of whipped double (heavy) cream or mascarpone at the end, or even some creamy Gorgonzola but this is a departure from tradition and frowned on by purists.

■ Vegetarians can omit the bone marrow and use vegetable broth and vegetarian Parmesan or Grana Padano cheese.

For the best flavour, only the best organic free-range chicken will do – the flavour is so superior to that of cheap supermarket birds. This is a great way to use up the leftover meat from your Sunday roast … and the carcass can be recycled, of course, to make another batch of chicken broth. Asparagus is a wonderful source of liver- and kidney-supporting nutrients, having naturally diuretic qualities. Shallots, being part of the allium family, are rich in sulphur, which is required by the liver for natural detoxification.

Summer chicken risotto with balsamic roasted shallots

SERVES 4

250 g/9 oz small shallots, peeled

3 tbsp olive oil

1 tbsp balsamic vinegar

1 bunch spring onions (scallions), trimmed and halved

150 g/5 oz thin asparagus spears, trimmed

2 small courgettes (zucchini), thinly sliced

15 g/½ oz unsalted butter

1 leek, trimmed and thinly sliced

250 g/9 oz/scant 1½ cups Arborio or Carnaroli risotto rice

100 ml/3½ fl oz/scant ½ cup white wine or dry vermouth

900 ml/1½ pints light chicken broth (see page 30)

300 g/10 oz cooked chicken (skinned and boned), shredded

juice of ½ lemon

30 g/1 oz fresh Parmesan, grated

salt and freshly ground black pepper

1 Preheat the oven to 180°C/350°F/gas mark 4. Arrange the shallots on a baking tray and drizzle over 2 tablespoons of the olive oil and the balsamic vinegar. Turn the shallots in the oil and vinegar to coat them all over, then transfer to the oven for 20–25 minutes until tender, golden brown and sticky.

2 Meanwhile, blanch the spring onions (scallions), asparagus and courgettes (zucchini) in a pan of boiling water for 2 minutes. Drain and refresh under cold running water, then drain again and set aside.

3 Heat the remaining olive oil and butter in a heavy-based wide pan and cook the leek over a low heat, stirring occasionally, until tender but not coloured. Add the rice and cook for 1–2 minutes, stirring, until it starts to crackle.

4 Pour in the wine or dry vermouth and cook over a medium heat until reduced and almost evaporated. Reduce the heat to a gentle simmer and start adding the hot broth, a ladleful at a time, stirring with each addition until all the liquid has been absorbed.

5 When all or most of the broth has been added and the rice is cooked and tender, gently stir in the chicken, lemon juice and blanched vegetables.

6 Take the pan off the heat and stir in the roasted shallots and Parmesan. Check the seasoning and leave to rest for 2–3 minutes before serving.

Or you can try this…

■ You can roast baby onions or wedges of red onion in the same way or sauté them in olive oil and butter in a small pan until caramelized and tender. Baby plum and cherry tomatoes can also be roasted like this and added to the risotto.

■ You can adapt this risotto to a wide range of spring and summer vegetables, including podded young peas, broad (fava) beans, mangetout (snow peas), sugar snap peas and baby spinach.

■ You can give the rice a more unctuous creamy consistency by stirring in a little crème fraîche or mascarpone with some grated lemon zest at the end.

Fragrant and scented with lemon, this simple dish of griddled chicken and couscous is really quick and easy to make. Couscous is made from tiny durum wheat granules and when cooked it should have a pleasantly light and fluffy texture. The flavour is quite bland so it is often combined with aromatic herbs and spices as well as lemon juice. People who follow a wheat-free diet can use barley couscous instead of the bulghur wheat-based varieties. The preserved lemons add an intensely citrus taste to this dish – always rinse them thoroughly before using as they are usually preserved in brine and can be very salty indeed.

Griddled chicken with scented lemon couscous

SERVES 4

250 g/9 oz/1½ cups couscous

400 ml/14 fl oz light chicken broth (see page 30)

4 free-range chicken breasts

2 tbsp olive oil, plus extra for drizzling

2 large courgettes (zucchini), sliced lengthwise into ribbons

grated zest and juice of 1 lemon

2 preserved lemons, drained and rinsed, pips removed and finely diced

1 bunch spring onions (scallions), finely chopped

1 small chilli, deseeded and diced

50 g/2 oz pine nuts, toasted

1 handful coriander (cilantro), chopped

1 handful flat-leaf parsley, chopped

salt and freshly ground black pepper

harissa paste, to serve

(ILLUSTRATED ON PAGES 138–139)

1 Put the couscous in a large heatproof bowl. Heat the chicken broth in a pan until it starts to boil, then pour over the couscous. Stir to combine, then cover with cling film (plastic wrap). Set aside for 10–15 minutes until the couscous has absorbed all the broth.

2 Meanwhile, cook the chicken breasts in a lightly oiled griddle pan over a medium heat for about 10 minutes each side until they are cooked right through and golden brown. Remove from the pan and set aside to rest.

3 Drizzle the courgette (zucchini) slices with a little oil. Set a clean ridged griddle pan over a medium heat and cook the courgettes, a few at a time, for about 1 minute each side until tender.

4 Fluff up the couscous with a fork and stir in the lemon zest and juice, preserved lemon, spring onions (scallions), chilli, pine nuts and herbs. Season with salt and gently fold in the grilled courgettes. Drizzle with olive oil.

5 Cut the grilled chicken breasts into thick slices and serve with the couscous. Hand the harissa around separately for people to help themselves as it is very hot indeed and should be used sparingly.

Or you can try this...

■ Grill some sliced aubergines (eggplants) or brightly coloured (bell) peppers and add to the couscous. Griddled or roasted baby plum tomatoes will add sweetness. Or experiment with different herbs: basil, Moroccan mint or chives.

■ Instead of harissa, serve with a hot Mexican salsa or creamy guacamole, or even some sweet chilli sauce and a dollop of natural yogurt.

■ This couscous is a delicious accompaniment to grilled lamb cutlets, chops, steaks or kebabs; or salmon, tuna or large prawns (jumbo shrimp); or even griddled halloumi cheese or tofu.

Spelt has long been underrated but it has an earthy, nutty flavour and coarse texture that can transform bakes and risottos. This ancient grain, which gets a mention in the Book of Exodus, makes a more digestible and nutritious alternative to commercially grown wheat, and it can be added to stews and casseroles or dressed and served lukewarm or cold as a salad.

Spelt with wild mushrooms

SERVES 4

3 tbsp olive oil

1 small onion, finely chopped

2 garlic cloves, crushed

200 g/7 oz pearled spelt, rinse and drained

125 ml/4 fl oz/scant ½ cup dry white wine

900 ml/1⅓ pints light chicken (see page 30) or vegetable top and tail broth (see page 50)

grated zest of 1 lemon

350 g/12 oz wild mushrooms, halved or quartered

50 g/2 oz unsalted butter

1 handful sage leaves

1–2 tbsp crème fraîche

salt and freshly ground black pepper

30 g/1 oz fresh Parmesan or Pecorino, grated

1 Heat 2 tablespoons olive oil in a wide heavy-based pan and cook the onion and garlic over a low heat, stirring occasionally, for about 6–8 minutes until soft but not coloured. Add the spelt and wine and cook, stirring continuously, until most of the liquid evaporates.

2 Meanwhile, heat the broth in another pan and bring to a gentle simmer. Add a ladleful to the spelt mixture and stir over a low heat until all the liquid has been absorbed. Keep adding the broth, a ladle at a time, and stirring in this way until the liquid has been absorbed and the spelt is cooked and tender – this will take about 20–25 minutes. Stir in the lemon zest and season to taste.

3 Cook the mushrooms in the remaining oil and half the butter in a frying pan until golden brown.

4 Melt the remaining butter in a clean frying pan and when it foams, add the sage leaves and cook briskly until they crisp. Remove immediately and drain on kitchen paper.

5 Stir the crème fraîche and mushrooms into the spelt mixture and divide between 4 serving plates. Scatter the sage leaves over the top and serve sprinkled with grated cheese.

Or you can try this...

■ If you can't get hold of wild mushrooms, meaty chestnut ones make a good substitute. Or you could even make this dish with soaked dried porcini. Add the soaking liquid to the broth.

■ Try stirring some shredded spinach, kale or cavolo nero into the spelt for the last couple of minutes of cooking. Or you can add cooked butternut squash, pumpkin, sweet potato, beetroot (beets), carrots, grilled onions or leeks.

■ Soft goat's cheese, feta, ricotta or creamy blue-veined Gorgonzola can be added to the finished dish. Have a play with different flavours.

A reassuring supper dish to make in the autumn when game is in season and wild mushrooms are plentiful – this is comfort food at its very best and it makes a single pheasant go a long way. Pheasant, being a lean game bird, has very little saturated fat, making this a deliciously satisfying meal, with all the protein and zinc that these birds have to offer helping to support immunity during the colder months of the year.

Pheasant and ceps risotto

SERVES 4

1 oven-ready plump pheasant

olive oil, for brushing

2 rashers pancetta

1 litre/1¾ pints game (see page 39) or dark rich chicken broth (see page 34)

15 g/½ oz dried porcini

30 g/1 oz unsalted butter

3 shallots, chopped

2 garlic cloves, crushed

225 g/8 oz ceps or wild mushrooms, halved or quartered

250 g/9 oz/scant 1½ cups Arborio or Carnaroli risotto rice

100 ml/3½ fl oz/scant ½ cup white wine or dry vermouth

a few cavolo nero leaves, sliced

30 g/1 oz fresh Parmesan, grated

grated zest of 1 lemon

3 tbsp crème fraîche

salt and freshly ground black pepper

1 Preheat the oven to 200°C/400°F/gas mark 6.

2 Put the pheasant in a roasting pan and brush it all over with olive oil. Drape the pancetta over the breast and roast in the preheated oven for about 45 minutes, until it is thoroughly cooked and the skin is crisp and golden brown. Remove and allow to cool before stripping the meat off the carcass – throw away the skin. Don't discard the carcass – you can use it to make another batch of broth. Cut the meat into small strips, crumble the pancetta into pieces and set aside.

3 Meanwhile, heat the game broth in a small pan until it is simmering. Put the dried porcini in a bowl and pour some of the simmering broth over them. Set aside to soak for about 15 minutes.

4 Heat the butter in a wide heavy-based pan and gently cook the shallots and garlic over a low heat, stirring occasionally, for about 8 minutes until softened but not coloured. Stir in the ceps or wild mushrooms and cook for 3–4 minutes until tender and golden.

5 Add the rice and stir for 2–3 minutes until the grains are glistening and it's starting to crackle. Pour in the wine or vermouth and let it bubble away until most of it has evaporated.

6 Start adding the simmering broth, a ladle at a time, together with the soaked porcini and the soaking liquid. Cook, stirring all the time, until the broth has been absorbed and then add some more. Keep adding the broth in this way, stirring all the time, until all or most of it has been used up and the rice is just tender but retains a little bite. This will take about 20 minutes.

7 Stir in the cavolo nero and let it wilt into the rice. Now add the pheasant, pancetta, grated Parmesan and lemon zest. Season to taste with salt and pepper, and stir in the crème fraîche. Stand for 2–3 minutes before serving.

Or you can try this…

■ You can use 2 roasted partridges instead of the pheasant, or even some cooked diced rabbit. In some rural areas of Italy it is not uncommon to make risotto with wild boar.

Rich in protein, high in fibre, cholesterol-free and gluten-free, quinoa has acquired the reputation of a 'super-food' in recent years. Because they taste somewhat bland, the grains are best cooked in some homemade vegetable or chicken bone broth – they absorb the flavour while retaining their shape and texture. Quinoa is actually known as a pseudo-grain as it is a seed, rather than a grain.

Quinoa with jerked prawns

SERVES 4

500 g/1 lb 2oz large raw shelled prawns (jumbo shrimp)

200 g/7 oz/scant 1¼ cups quinoa

500 ml/16 fl oz shellfish (see page 47) or vegetable top and tail broth (see page 50)

3 tbsp fruity green olive oil

juice of 1–2 limes

1 bunch spring onions (scallions), diced

1 small bunch coriander (cilantro), chopped

1 large ripe avocado, peeled, stoned (pitted) and diced

salt and freshly ground black pepper

For the jerk seasoning:

2 tsp allspice berries

2 tsp black peppercorns

a good pinch of ground nutmeg

a good pinch of ground cinnamon

leaves stripped from 4 sprigs thyme

1 shallot, diced

2 garlic cloves, crushed

2.5 cm/1 in piece fresh root ginger, peeled and diced

2 Scotch bonnet chillies, deseeded and diced

2 tsp brown sugar

1 tbsp soy sauce

juice of 1 lime

1 To make the seasoning, crush the allspice and peppercorns with a pestle and mortar. Put them in a blender with all the other ingredients and blitz to a paste. Transfer the seasoning to a bowl and add the prawns (jumbo shrimp). Turn them over in the marinade until coated. Cover and leave in the refrigerator for at least 30 minutes.

2 Rinse the quinoa under cold running water, then drain. Heat the broth in a pan and when it starts to boil, add the quinoa. Reduce the heat, cover the pan and simmer gently for about 15 minutes until tender and most of the broth has been absorbed. You will know when it is cooked because the 'sprout' or 'tail' will pop out of the seed.

3 Turn off the heat and leave the quinoa to steam in the pan for 5–8 minutes before draining off any excess liquid. Fluff it up with a fork.

4 Add 2 tablespoons olive oil and the lime juice to the quinoa and mix gently together. Season to taste with salt and pepper.

5 Cook the prawns in their marinade in the remaining oil in a frying pan or on a griddle or barbecue for 1–2 minutes each side until they are pink and succulent.

6 Divide the quinoa between 4 plates and garnish with the spring onions (scallions), coriander (cilantro) and avocado. Arrange the prawns on top and serve immediately.

Or you can try this...

■ Griddled jerked chicken breasts cut into thick slices make an alternative to prawns (shrimp). Or you could turn some salmon fillets in a teriyaki marinade before grilling them and serving with the quinoa.

■ For a vegetarian alternative, try serving the quinoa topped with roasted red or yellow beetroot (beets), steamed purple-sprouting broccoli, wilted spinach or sautéed mushrooms.

■ Jewel-like pomegranate seeds, diced mango or papaya, orange segments, cherry tomatoes, chopped parsley, chives, dill or basil can all be folded into quinoa to make a delicious warm salad.

Variations on this risotto are served all around the Italian coastline, using whatever fish is local and available. The most important ingredient of all is freshness — the fresher the fish and shellfish you use, the better the flavour of the finished dish. All shellfish are a great source of zinc and selenium, which support the immune system and natural metabolic rate, making this a slimmer's dream!

Risotto ai frutti di mare

SERVES 4

450 g/1 lb small clams in their shells, scrubbed

25 g/1 oz unsalted butter, plus extra for finishing

2 tbsp olive oil

1 onion, finely chopped

1 small fennel bulb, trimmed and thinly sliced

2 garlic cloves, crushed

350 g/12 oz fresh or frozen and thawed squid, cut into pieces

a pinch of chilli flakes or powder

250 g/9 oz/scant 1½ cups Arborio or Carnaroli risotto rice

125 ml/4 fl oz/generous ½ cup dry white wine or dry vermouth

1 litre/1¾ pints hot simmering white fish bone (see page 43) or shellfish broth (see page 47)

a pinch of saffron threads

200 g/7 oz baby plum tomatoes, halved

350 g/12 oz large raw prawns (jumbo shrimp)

juice of 1 lemon

salt and freshly ground black pepper

1 small bunch parsley, chopped

1 Put the clams in a large pan with a little water. Place over a medium heat for about 5 minutes, shaking the pan occasionally, until the clams have opened — discard any that stay closed. Remove about half the clams from their shells and set aside together with the remaining ones in their shells.

2 Heat the butter and olive oil in a heavy-based wide pan and cook the onion, fennel and garlic over a low heat, stirring occasionally, for 8–10 minutes until tender but not coloured.

3 Add the prepared squid and cook gently for about 8 minutes, stirring often, until tender. Stir in the chilli and the rice and cook for a few more minutes until the grains are crackling. Pour in the wine or vermouth and turn up the heat. Cook rapidly for 2–3 minutes until reduced and almost evaporated.

4 Reduce the heat to a gentle simmer and add a ladleful of the hot simmering broth with the saffron and cook gently, stirring, until all the liquid has been absorbed. Add another ladle of broth and continue stirring and adding more in this way until the rice is tender but not too soft, about 20 minutes.

5 Stir in the tomatoes, prawns (shrimp) and reserved clams. Cook for a few more minutes until the prawns turn pink and the tomatoes start to soften.

6 Remove from the heat and season to taste with salt and pepper. Stir in the lemon juice, parsley and a knob of butter. Cover the pan and set aside to rest for 5 minutes before serving.

Or you can try this…

■ You can add any fish or shellfish to this risotto – a cooked dressed crab, langoustines, chunks of cooked lobster meat plus the cracked claws, scallops, mussels or pieces of fish … even a packet of frozen fruits de mer if you're in a hurry.

■ Parmesan is not usually served with seafood and fish risottos in Italy but you can rebel and sprinkle some over the top if you like. For a creamy texture, stir in a little double (heavy) cream or crème fraîche with the parsley and butter.

Peas are one of the richest sources of vitamin C, making this a healthy and light risotto. A Venetian speciality, it is best made in late spring and early summer when very young peas are in season and particularly sweet and tender. During the Venetian Republic it was deemed so special that it was only served on 25th April, St Mark's Day, as decreed by the Doge. It's the simplest way to make a risotto-type dish if you don't like standing over a hot stove, adding the broth gradually and stirring away.

Risi e bisi

SERVES 4

900 g/2 lb very young peas in their pods

1 litre/1¾ pints vegetable top and tail (see page 50) or light chicken broth (see page 30)

30 g/1 oz unsalted butter

2 tbsp olive oil

2 garlic cloves, thinly sliced

1 bunch spring onions (scallions), finely chopped

2 sage leaves

200 g/7 oz/generous 1 cup Arborio or Carnaroli risotto rice

100 g/3½ oz pea shoots or baby spinach leaves

grated zest of ½ lemon

50 g/2 oz fresh Parmesan, grated, plus extra for sprinkling

long thin strips of lean prosciutto (visible fat removed), to serve (optional)

1 Remove the peas from the pods and set aside. Place the pods in a large saucepan with the vegetable or chicken broth. Bring to the boil, then reduce the heat and simmer for 30 minutes. Strain the broth, pressing down on the softened pods, through a colander or sieve. Pour the hot broth back into the pan and keep it at a gentle simmer.

2 Heat the butter and oil in a clean pan and cook the garlic and spring onions (scallions) over a low heat for about 5 minutes until tender but not coloured. Stir in the sage leaves, podded peas and rice and cook for 2 minutes, stirring until all the rice grains are glistening.

3 Add the simmering broth and bring to the boil. Reduce the heat and simmer for 15–20 minutes, or until the rice is tender but still retains some bite (al dente). The overall consistency should be slightly more liquid than a risotto but not soupy. This is eaten with a fork, not a spoon.

4 Stir in the pea shoots or baby spinach together with the lemon juice and parsley. Simmer gently over a very low heat until the green leaves start to wilt, then stir in the Parmesan.

5 Serve the Risi e bisi in shallow bowls or deep plates, sprinkled with Parmesan and strips of prosciutto.

Or you can try this...

■ Simmering the pea pods first in the broth gives it more flavour and colour. In Venice, sometimes they are liquidized or puréed together to produce a thicker vibrant green broth. You can use sugar snap peas if you can't get fresh young peas but frozen peas don't cut it in this dish!

■ Pancetta cubes can be cooked in the oil and butter with the onions or used as a garnish instead of the prosciutto. You can replace the spring onions (scallions) with a chopped onion or 3 shallots.

■ If you have no pea shoots or spinach, stir in plenty of chopped flat-leaf parsley and snipped chives at the end.

The thin stems of asparagus are ideal for using in risotto — better to keep the fatter ones for serving with melted butter or a lemony vinaigrette. When preparing the asparagus, discard any dry, shrivelled or slimy stems. Cut off the woody ends and, if necessary, pare the rougher lower section of the stems with a potato peeler. Remember that all herbs have their own distinct taste, and you may prefer to use only one or two of those listed below. Always use fresh herbs when making this risotto — they really do make a huge difference to the taste as well as the nutritional value.

Asparagus, lemon and herb-flecked risotto

SERVES 4

50 g/2 oz unsalted butter, plus extra for finishing

3 shallots, finely chopped

450 g/1 lb asparagus, trimmed and cut into 5 cm/2 in lengths

250 g/9 oz/scant 1½ cups Arborio or Carnaroli risotto rice

125 ml/4 fl oz/generous ½ cup white wine or dry vermouth

1 litre/1¾ pints vegetable top and tail (see page 50) or dark rich chicken broth (see page 34)

grated zest and juice of 2 lemons

1 small handful each of chervil, chives, parsley and tarragon, finely chopped

salt and freshly ground black pepper

30 g/1 oz fresh Parmesan, grated, plus extra for sprinkling

1 Heat the butter in a heavy-based wide pan and cook the shallots over a low heat, stirring occasionally, until softened but not coloured. Add the asparagus and cook for 1–2 minutes.

2 Meanwhile, heat the broth to simmering point in another pan.

3 Add the rice to the shallots and asparagus and keep stirring gently until all the grains are glistening and coated with butter. Pour in the wine or vermouth and cook until most of the liquid has evaporated.

4 Add a ladle of broth and stir until it has all been absorbed by the rice, then add another ladleful. Keep adding and stirring in this way until all or most of the broth has been used up and the rice is plump and tender with a little bite.

5 Stir in the grated lemon zest and juice and the chopped herbs. Season to taste with salt and pepper. Beat in the Parmesan and a knob of butter and serve.

Or you can try this…

■ For a more creamy textured risotto, stir in 4 tablespoons crème fraîche before adding the Parmesan and butter.

■ If you wish, you can top this risotto with some grilled large prawns (jumbo shrimp), sliced griddled chicken breast or crisply fried rashers (slices) of pancetta. Or garnish with Parmesan crisps (see page 81).

■ You can make this risotto into a vegetarian feast by adding other spring and summer green vegetables and herbs: pea pods and shoots, young baby leeks, purple sprouting broccoli, spinach, sorrel, rocket (arugula), mint and basil.

■ You can use up cold leftover risotto by moulding it into small sticky balls. Dip them into beaten egg and coat with fresh white breadcrumbs before shallow-frying in olive oil until crisp and golden brown. If you wish, mould the rice around a small piece of mozzarella, which oozes seductively when you bite into these savoury hot arancini.

The radicchio used in this distinctively coloured risotto, which is often served in Venice and the Veneto region, imparts a slightly bitter taste, beloved of the Italians. However, it is less bitter cooked than eaten raw in a salad. Unless you're vegetarian, use chicken bone broth to make this colourful dish. The more gelatinous broth produces a risotto with a really silky, creamy texture. Radicchio is rich in potassium (great for people with an elevated blood pressure to balance sodium levels in the body) and beta-carotene to support the immune system.

Radicchio di Treviso risotto

SERVES 6

450 g/1 lb radicchio Trevisano
85 g/3 oz unsalted butter
1 onion, chopped
2 garlic cloves, crushed
250 g/9 oz/scant 1½ cups Arborio or Carnaroli risotto rice
125 ml/4 fl oz/generous ½ cup dry vermouth
1 litre/1¾ pints vegetable top and tail (see page 50) or light chicken broth (see page 30)
olive oil for drizzling
50 g/2 oz fresh Parmesan, grated
salt and freshly ground black pepper
a few drops of aged balsamic vinegar (optional)

1 Prepare the radicchio: reserve a few leaves for the garnish and cut the rest crosswise into strips.

2 Heat half the butter in a wide heavy-based pan and cook the onion and garlic over a low heat, stirring occasionally, for about 8 minutes until softened but not coloured. Stir in the rice and strips of radicchio. Keep stirring for 1–2 minutes until the rice is glistening and coated in the butter.

3 Tip in the vermouth and cook for a few minutes until most of the liquid has evaporated. Now add a ladle of simmering broth and stir until it has been absorbed. Add another ladleful and keep stirring and adding in this way until all or most of the broth has been used and the rice is tender but still retains a little bite.

4 Meanwhile, place a griddle pan over a medium heat. Sprinkle the remaining radicchio leaves with olive oil and some seasoning and cook them on the griddle for 6–8 minutes until they are tender and starting to brown at the edges.

5 Beat the rest of the butter and the Parmesan into the risotto and check the seasoning. Cover and let it rest for 5 minutes before serving topped with the chargrilled radicchio and drizzled with balsamic vinegar (if using).

Or you can try this...

■ If you can't get hold of any radicchio di Treviso you can use slender-leaved red chicory (Belgian endive) instead but the colour will not be so vibrant. Using red wine instead of vermouth will enhance the reddish hue of the finished dish.

■ Bitter greens also make a delicious risotto – experiment with strongly flavoured rocket (arugula), mustard greens or kale.

■ Some people soak the radicchio in cold water and then drain and dry it on kitchen paper to remove the bitterness before adding it to the risotto, but we love the bitter taste. It helps to offset the starchiness of the rice, the creamy, buttery texture and the richly flavoured chicken broth.

Don't be put off by the shocking pink colour of this risotto — it has a wonderfully elemental and earthy flavour. It can be eaten on its own, or without the cheese and makes the perfect accompaniment to oily fish, such as grilled mackerel or sardines. The beta-carotene and iron in the beetroot (beets) make this risotto a great way for vegetarians to get these harder-to-absorb nutrients; vegans can simply omit the goat's cheese.

Beetroot and goat's cheese risotto

SERVES 4

300 g/10 oz raw beetroot (beets), peeled and coarsely grated

1 litre/1¾ pints vegetable top and tail broth (see page 50)

2 tbsp olive oil

25 g/1 oz unsalted butter, plus extra for finishing

1 onion, chopped

2 garlic cloves, crushed

200 g/7 oz/generous 1 cup Arborio or Carnaroli risotto rice

100 ml/3½ fl oz/scant ½ cup red wine

100 g/3½ oz soft goat's cheese

salt and freshly ground black pepper

1 small bunch dill or chives, snipped

(ILLUSTRATED ON PAGES 156–157)

1 Put the beetroot (beets) in a large pan with the broth and heat it to a gentle simmer. Leave it simmer gently while you start making the risotto.

2 Heat the olive oil and butter in a wide heavy-based pan and cook the onion and garlic for about 8 minutes, stirring occasionally, until softened but not coloured. Stir in the rice and cook for a couple of minutes until all the grains are glistening.

3 Turn up the heat and stir in the red wine. Cook for a few minutes until most of the liquid has evaporated. Add a ladle of the simmering broth and cook, stirring, over a low heat until all the liquid has been absorbed. Keep adding the broth and grated beetroot, a ladleful at a time, in this way until all the broth and beetroot have been used up and the rice is tender and al dente.

4 Season the risotto with salt and pepper and beat in a knob of butter. Gently stir in the goat's cheese or divide into small pieces or spoonfuls, depending on how soft it is, and scatter over the top.

5 Sprinkle with the snipped herbs and serve immediately.

Or you can try this...

■ Omit the goat's cheese and serve each portion of risotto with one of the following: some diced feta, a spoonful of soured cream, thick natural Greek yogurt, mascarpone or even some horseradish cream.

■ Another way to cook the beetroot (beets) is to roast them in the oven, then cut some of them into small cubes and blitz the rest to a purée. Mix both into the cooked risotto. Or use halved roasted beets as a garnish.

■ In California, yellow beets are sometimes used to make a wonderfully sweet and golden risotto. Prepare and cook them in the same way as the recipe above and serve with a simple crisp green salad.

Slightly crunchy and nutty-tasting bulghur wheat is the star of many Middle Eastern and Mediterranean dishes where it's used in soups, stews and salads, as well as for stuffing vegetables. A good source of protein and minerals, it is best known as the main ingredient in tabbouleh. You can use fine- or medium-grained bulghur wheat to make this – the fine sort is more authentic but we prefer the texture and chewiness of the medium variety. Anyone following a gluten-free diet can make this dish with quinoa instead of bulghur wheat.

Tabbouleh with griddled raddichio and goat's cheese

SERVES 4

50 g/2 oz sultanas (golden raisins)
200 g/7 oz/scant 1½ cups bulghur wheat
250 ml/9 fl oz vegetable top and tail broth (see page 50)
1 red onion, finely chopped
225 g/8 oz ripe baby plum tomatoes, diced
1 bunch flat-leaf parsley, finely chopped
a few sprigs mint, finely chopped
juice of 2 lemons
4 tbsp fruity green olive oil, plus extra for oiling
30 g/1 oz hazelnuts
4 small radicchio heads, cut in half or quarters lengthwise
200 g/7 oz soft goat's cheese, cut into pieces
salt and freshly ground black pepper
seeds of ½ pomegranate

1 Put the sultanas (golden raisins) in a small bowl and pour over some hot water. Leave to soak for at least 10 minutes until they plump up. Drain and set aside.

2 Put the bulghur wheat and broth in a pan and bring to the boil. Reduce the heat, cover the pan and simmer for 5 minutes. Take the pan off the heat and leave in the covered pan to continue cooking for at least another 5 minutes until the grains of bulghur wheat are tender and have absorbed most of the broth.

3 Transfer the bulghur wheat to a large bowl and mix in the drained sultanas, red onion, tomatoes, herbs, lemon juice and olive oil. Season to taste.

4 Place a dry frying pan over a medium heat and add the hazelnuts. Toast for about 2 minutes, stirring frequently, until they start to turn golden brown – don't let them burn. Remove immediately.

5 Lightly oil a griddle pan and place over a medium heat. Add the radicchio when it's hot and cook for 1–2 minutes only until it's just starting to wilt and get slightly charred.

6 Divide the radicchio between 4 serving plates and add the tabbouleh. Dot with the goat's cheese and sprinkle with the toasted hazelnuts and pomegranate seeds.

Or you can try this...

■ You can griddle Belgian endives (red or white) instead of radicchio. They have the same bitter flavour and crisp texture. Toasted pine nuts, pumpkin and sunflower seeds can be substituted for the hazelnuts.

■ Add some fresh fruit, such as sliced pears, blood orange or ruby red grapefruit segments, to the tabbouleh. It's unorthodox but delicious and helps in your quest to get your five-a-day!

■ Instead of goat's cheese, you could use cubes of feta, griddled halloumi or large shavings of Parmesan or Pecorino cheese. Drizzle with a little balsamic vinegar for piquant sweetness.

This versatile dish is much easier to cook than a classic risotto as all the broth is added at once and the barley only needs an occasional stir. It absorbs the flavour of the broth as it cooks and swells to a tender plumpness. Pearl barley is one of the richest wholegrain sources of zinc, which is necessary for rebuilding and repairing our bodies, and a healthy immune system. This is a superb source of zinc for vegetarians.

Pearl barley with roasted vegetables and tahini sauce

SERVES 4

2 red (bell) peppers, deseeded and sliced

1 red onion, peeled and cut into wedges

1 large sweet potato, peeled and cut into chunks

3 sprigs rosemary

4 tbsp olive oil, plus extra for drizzling

2 shallots, finely chopped

1 tbsp fennel seeds

1 tsp cumin seeds

1 pinch dried chilli flakes

300 g/10 oz/1½ cups pearl barley

900 ml/1½ pints vegetable top and tail broth (see page 50)

grated zest and juice of 1 large lemon

3 tbsp chopped flat-leaf parsley

85 g/3 oz baby spinach leaves

salt and freshly ground black pepper

For the tahini yogurt sauce:

125 ml/4 fl oz/generous ½ cup natural Greek yogurt

1 tbsp tahini

1 garlic clove, crushed

a squeeze of lemon juice

2 spring onions (scallions), thinly sliced

clear honey, to drizzle

1 Preheat the oven to 200°C/400°F/gas mark 6.

2 Place the red (bell) peppers, red onion and sweet potato on a baking tray. Tuck the rosemary sprigs in between the vegetables. Drizzle over 2 tablespoons of the olive oil and season with salt and pepper. Roast in the preheated oven for about 30 minutes, turning the vegetables once or twice, until they are just tender. Remove the rosemary and set the vegetables aside.

3 Meanwhile, heat the remaining olive oil in a heavy-based pan and cook the shallots over a low heat, stirring occasionally, for about 5 minutes until softened but not coloured. Stir in the seeds and chilli flakes and cook gently for 1–2 minutes until they start to release their aroma. Now stir in the pearl barley and cook for 1 minute until the grains are glistening with oil

4 Add the hot broth and simmer gently for about 30 minutes, stirring frequently to stop the barley sticking to the bottom of the pan. When the barley is tender and al dente and all the broth has been absorbed, add the lemon zest and juice and parsley. Stir in the spinach and let it wilt into the barley mixture. Season to taste with salt and pepper.

5 While the barley is cooking, make the tahini yogurt sauce in a small bowl. Mix together the yogurt, tahini, garlic and lemon juice until well blended. Sprinkle with spring onions (scallions) and drizzle with a little honey.

6 Divide the barley mixture between 4 serving plates and arrange the roasted vegetables on top. Serve immediately with the tahini yogurt sauce.

Or you can try this...

■ Roast a colourful assortment of vegetables: in summer, try yellow and green (bell) peppers, courgettes (zucchini), aubergine (eggplant), fennel bulb and baby plum or cherry tomatoes; in winter, mushrooms, butternut squash, parsnips, carrots and beetroot (beets).

■ Or sauté some sliced wild mushrooms and pancetta or smoked bacon cubes in a little olive oil until golden brown and mix into the cooked barley.

SAUCES

A classic Bordelaise sauce is made with veal broth but veal has gone out of fashion and bones are hard to come by, so you can make this delicious alternative with beef bone broth. The sauce is named after the Bordeaux region of France, which is revered for its fine red wine, often known as claret. This is quite a rich sauce with a very distinctive well-rounded flavour – perfect for turning a humble grilled steak into something special. You can make it a day or two in advance and store in a covered container in the fridge until needed. Reheat to serve.

Bordelaise sauce

MAKES ABOUT 300 ML/½ PINT

2 shallots, finely diced

1 garlic clove, crushed

6 black peppercorns, crushed

200 ml/7 fl oz/generous ¾ cup red Bordeaux wine

a dash of sherry vinegar or red wine vinegar

300 ml/½ pint classic beef bone broth (see page 18)

1 sprig fresh thyme

30 g/1 oz unsalted butter, diced

salt and freshly ground black pepper

1 Combine the shallots, garlic, peppercorns, red wine and vinegar in a saucepan and cook over a medium heat until the vegetables have softened.

2 Turn up the heat and cook until the mixture is reduced and syrupy.

3 Add the beef broth and thyme and simmer for 15–20 minutes until the sauce reduces to about two-thirds of its original volume. It should be thick enough to coat the back of a spoon.

4 Remove from the heat and strain through a conical sieve into a clean saucepan. Season to taste.

5 Off the heat, whisk in the butter until it is well blended and the sauce is shiny.

What you can do with this...

■ Some chefs like to add diced bone marrow to the Bordelaise. Put it in a saucepan and cover with cold water. Bring to the boil, then turn off the heat and set aside for less than 1 minute before draining and adding it to the finished sauce. Alternatively, you can use rich marrow bone broth (see page 22) instead of beef bone broth to make the sauce.

■ Serve this sauce as an accompaniment to steak and beef fillet as well as roast sirloin or rib of beef. It also goes well with roasted pork tenderloin.

■ You might be surprised to learn that in France it is sometimes served with grilled or oven-baked mullet and sea bass. However, a white version made with white wine and white fish bone broth with tarragon instead of thyme is more usual with fish, especially sole. A dash of cognac is often added instead of vinegar.

This is one of Escoffier's five 'mother sauces', the classic brown sauce that was used as a base for so many others, including demi-glace, Bercy, Chasseur and Madeira sauces. In the past it was always made with broth made from roasted veal bones but now most chefs make a lighter version with chicken or beef broth, which is more in keeping with our contemporary approach to less rich, healthy food. It's not difficult to make – it always starts with a 'mirepoix' of diced onion, celery and carrot cooked slowly in butter, and a simple 'roux' (a cooked mixture of flour and fat) is used as a thickening agent. You may wish to make this with quinoa, rice or chickpea (gram) flour if you are fastidious about a gluten-free diet.

Espagnole sauce

MAKES ABOUT 900 ML/1½ PINTS

60 g/2 oz unsalted butter
1 onion, diced
1 stick celery, diced
1 carrot, diced
30 g/1 oz plain (all-purpose) flour
30 g/1 oz tomato purée (paste)
900 ml/1½ pints hot dark rich chicken (see page 34) or classic beef bone broth (see page 18)
1 bay leaf
a few black peppercorns

1 Melt the butter in a saucepan over a low heat and cook the onion, celery and carrot, stirring occasionally, for 6–8 minutes until tender and golden.

2 Stir in the flour and cook over a low heat for a few minutes until the roux turns brown – take care not to let it burn or you will have to start again.

3 Start adding the hot broth slowly, whisking vigorously all the time, until it is thoroughly incorporated and there are no lumps.

4 Stir in the tomato purée, bay leaf and peppercorns and bring to the boil. Reduce the heat to a bare simmer and cook gently, stirring occasionally, until reduced to about two-thirds of the original volume. This may take 30–45 minutes.

5 Strain through a fine mesh sieve and serve immediately or cool and use as a base for other sauces. If you wish, store in containers or freezer bags and freeze until required.

What you can do with this...

■ You can play with this basic recipe by adding chopped, skinned and deseeded tomatoes, garlic or a little white wine or Madeira for extra flavour.

■ To make a highly flavoured demi-glace sauce, heat equal quantities of Espagnole sauce and chicken or veal broth in a saucepan and cook until reduced by half. Strain through a fine mesh sieve until it's really smooth.

■ Serve this sauce as a savoury gravy with roasted meat, especially beef, veal and lamb – it adds the finishing touches to the Sunday roast. Or pour a little pool on a serving plate and add a griddled juicy steak and mushrooms.

This light lemon sauce is served with chicken, meat, fish and vegetables throughout Greece and its archipelago of islands. With its fresh, sharp taste, avgolemono manages to be robust yet delicate at the same time. Ideally, it should be made in a double boiler but if you don't have one, just suspend a basin over a pan of simmering water.

Avgolemono sauce

MAKES 300 ML/½ PINT

300 ml/½ pint dark rich chicken broth (see page 34)
3 eggs
juice of 1 large lemon

1 Heat the chicken broth in a pan to a gentle simmer. Heat some water in the bottom of a double boiler or another pan over a low heat.

2 Break the eggs into the top of a double boiler or a large heatproof bowl and beat with an electric whisk. Beat in the lemon juice.

3 Slowly add the hot broth to the egg and lemon mixture, beating continuously.

4 Place over the pan of simmering water and continue beating or stirring until the sauce is smooth and thick. As soon as it's the right consistency, take it off the heat to prevent it curdling. To be on the safe side, you can quickly dip the base of the top of the double boiler or bowl into some cold water to halt the cooking process and cool it.

What you can do with this...

■ Serve this sauce with roast, grilled or poached chicken, lamb cutlets or kebabs, lamb or veal meatballs, grilled or oven-baked white fish, boiled vegetables or dolmades – rice and lamb stuffed vine leaves that are cooked in chicken broth.

■ A lighter, thinner version is a delicious soup made with 1 litre/1¾ pints chicken broth, 3 eggs and a large lemon. A little rice or orzo (pasta shaped like grains of rice) is added to the soup and cooked until tender.

■ Alternatively you can make an avgolemono fish soup by substituting white fish bone broth for chicken broth and adding chunks of white fish and potato.

You may know this better as the sweet-and-sour orange sauce that is usually served with duck and game. It derives its name from the Provençal word for the bitter Seville-type oranges that are used for making marmalade. Its sharpness cuts through the fatty succulence of duck, complementing it perfectly. Traditionally, it is made with veal broth but it works well with chicken broth, too. The vitamin C in the fresh oranges is great for supporting the immune system, especially if you are lucky enough to have picked the oranges from your own tree! For a healthier sweetener, you can use agave syrup instead of sugar.

Bigarade sauce

MAKES ABOUT 350 ML/12 FL OZ

4 Seville oranges
20 g/¾ oz caster (superfine) sugar
2 tbsp red wine vinegar or balsamic vinegar
350 ml/12 fl oz light chicken broth (see page 30)
25 g/1 oz butter, diced
salt and freshly ground black pepper

1 Remove the zest from 2 of the oranges and cut into fine julienne strips. Drop them into a pan of boiling water and blanch for 1 minute. Remove with a slotted spoon, drain and set aside. Meanwhile, juice all the oranges.

2 Heat the sugar and vinegar in a saucepan over a low heat, stirring until the sugar dissolves. Cook gently until it starts to turn golden and caramelize. Keep an eye on it and be careful not to let it burn.

3 Stir in the broth and orange juice and bring to the boil. Reduce the heat and simmer gently for about 30–40 minutes, skimming the surface from time to time to remove any scum, until the sauce reduces and coats the back of a spoon.

4 Strain with a conical strainer into a clean saucepan. Beat in the butter until the sauce is glossy, then stir in the strips of orange zest. Serve immediately or leave to cool and reheat just before serving.

What you can do with this...

■ When bitter Seville oranges are out of season, use the juice of 3 sweet oranges and 1 juicy lemon instead.

■ The sauce can also be made with duck broth – make it in the same way as chicken bone broth using duck bones and wings – or even beef bone broth, although this will give a slightly darker colour and richer flavour.

■ This sauce is usually served with grilled duck breasts or roast duck, but it is equally delicious with guinea fowl, pot-roasted pheasant and other game birds.

■ And you don't have to be a traditionalist and stick to duck – venison, sautéed sweetbreads, calves' liver, grilled pork steaks or chops or even a boiled gammon joint can all be enhanced by this bitter-sweet sauce.

This classic white sauce is one of the celebrated French chef Auguste Escoffier's five 'mother sauces' that can be served on their own or used as a base for other sauces. This chicken velouté is made with chicken bone broth but you can substitute white fish bone broth (see page 43) if you're serving it with fish or shellfish. The important thing is to use a light broth, not one made with roasted bones. Velouté is simple to make, starting with the classic roux that is the foundation of so many sauces. For all the variations on this sauce that involve a roux, use chickpea flour, quinoa flour or rice flour to make a gluten-free version should that be your nutritional choice.

Velouté sauce

MAKES ABOUT 400 ML/14 FL OZ

30 g/1 oz butter
30 g/1 oz plain (all-purpose) flour
400 ml/14 fl oz light chicken broth
(see page 30)
salt and freshly ground black pepper

1 Heat the butter in a heavy-based pan over a low heat until melted. Take the pan off the heat and stir in the flour with a wooden spoon until combined.

2 Return the pan to the heat and keep stirring for 2 minutes until smooth. Be careful not to let the mixture brown. The pale golden paste should smell toasted and vaguely nutty.

3 Increase the heat to medium and add about one-third of the chicken broth. Using a small whisk, beat the mixture until well combined with no lumps. Add some more broth and whisk well, then beat in the remaining broth until smooth.

4 Reduce the heat to very low and simmer gently for about 10 minutes, stirring occasionally, until thickened, velvety and smooth. Season to taste. If a skin forms, remove it. To ensure the sauce is very smooth, pass it through a fine mesh strainer or conical sieve before serving.

What you can do with this ...

■ To add flavour, stir in 2–3 tablespoons of dry sherry or white vermouth. Or add some finely chopped cooked spinach and cream, or some roasted garlic or diced cooked wild or cultivated mushrooms. For a creamier, richer version of the basic sauce, enrich it with egg yolks and double (heavy) cream.

■ Serve the warm chicken velouté with poached or sautéed chicken breasts; a fish-based velouté complements poached, grilled or fried delicate white fish, such as sole, flounder or plaice fillets.

■ When making a chicken and ham pie or chicken, leek and mushroom pie, mix the cooked vegetables (onions, leeks, mushrooms) with the chicken velouté sauce, then stir in the chicken and/or ham before topping with pastry. You can make a fish pie with a fish velouté in the same way, adding chunks of cooked salmon, white or smoked fish and prawns.

INDEX

AUTHORS' ACKNOWLEDGEMENTS

We would like to thank Jacqui Small for believing in this project and taking a punt on it like the true publisher she is. And also her wonderful team: Maggie Town for her beautiful and intelligent design, Lisa Linder for her stunning photography, Jennifer Joyce for her creative food styling, Daniel Hurst for his impeccable editing, and all those behind the scenes who have worked so hard to bring this book together.

Special thanks also go to Vicki's sister Shelley and her family who made the task of writing so much easier and without whom this book would not have happened.